THE SECRETS
TO MARKETING

&

AUTOMATING
YOUR LAW PRACTICE

A LAWYER'S GUIDE TO CREATING SYSTEMS, GETTING CLIENTS, & BECOMING A LEGAL RAINMAKER

EDITED BY **DAVID BITTON**
FOREWORD BY **ROBERT AMBROGI**

The materials in this book are for informational purposes
only and not legal advice. Please contact an attorney for legal
advice or any ethics and rules regarding legal marketing. Use
of and access to this book or any of the content and links
contained do not create an attorney-client relationship between
PracticePanther, any of the contributors, and the reader.
The opinions expressed in this book are the opinions of the
individual contributors and may not reflect the opinions of
PracticePanther.

ISBN:1985211289
ISBN-13:9781985211285

DEDICATION

This book is dedicated to the Panther family. Thank you for putting your heart and soul into helping thousands of law firms worldwide take their practices to the next level.

The legal industry is in a better place thanks to you.

To many more years of continued growth, success, optimization, and automation!

CONTENTS

LAW FIRM PRODUCTIVITY & AUTOMATION

PROTECTING YOUR FIRM

PREFACE

About This Book

By David Bitton, *Co-Founder & CEO, PracticePanther.com*

The legal industry is changing faster than ever before. More people are graduating law school, and starting their own firms after graduating. These attorneys in their 20s have unprecedented knowledge and experience in using the latest social media apps to market and promote themselves and their firms. There's also a new wave of legal consumers who are demanding immediate service, quality websites, excellent reviews online, great branding, and more attention.

With that comes the rise of more online services that cater to consumers who wish to find the answers themselves, look up legal advice on their own, download legal forms, and do as much as possible without speaking to an attorney.

The challenges to starting, growing, and maintaining a successful law firm are greater than ever. When demand is less than the supply of law firms, lawyers start to have a problem. If you wish to succeed in this new industry saturated with legal tech, you must be willing, able, and prepared to adapt and bring your firm up to speed with today's technology and consumer demands. Luckily, this book will hopefully help you accomplish all these goals and more.

I have personally met and spoken with thousands of attorneys in the last few years. I've noticed a few patterns of behavior amongst the most successful lawyers who were able to quickly scale up and grow their practices. It's been incredible seeing some of our own members going from three people in the firm to over thirty in under two years. Most of what they were doing seemed fairly obvious, and it always puzzled me why more people weren't doing as well as thy were. With a little guidance, I'm confident most law firms can be just as successful, if not more.

I also observed the law firms that needed serious help. The ones that ordered free business cards online, made their websites themselves, and just didn't know anything about marketing or how to grow a business. The truth is, it's not their fault. Most law schools don't teach or prepare you on opening your own firm. Even when working for someone else, you're not exactly focused on the marketing aspect of the business. There are of course, many similarities between marketing a law firm and any other business. However, there are also many differences, both practically and ethically, that you need to be aware of.

We've rounded up the legal industry's top experts and consultants and asked them to provide their single best piece of content for how to start, grow, market, and automate your firm. After reading through them, I am blown away by the amount of knowledge and industry trade secrets they've offered to give away for free.

This book is divided into four sections:
1. Starting and growing your own firm
2. Social media, marketing, and SEO (search engine optimization)
3. Law firm productivity and automation
4. Protecting your firm

If you already have your own practice, and even if you have 50 attorneys in your firm, I still highly recommend reading the first section that deals with opening your own firm. It holds countless great tips and insights that you can still implement today.

I recommend going through each chapter and marking or highlighting the important tasks you wish to accomplish. The only way you're going to implement them is if you add the action items into a date and time on your calendar and start executing right away.

If you're reading this, congratulations! It means you've already taken the first step, and you're in the top tier of attorneys who care about growing their law firms. I know it's not easy to set aside time for working on the business of your law firm, but the sooner you start, the sooner you will see results.

I am so excited for you to read and implement the advice in this book, and I'm confident that it will help take your firm to the next level. Our entire team at PracticePanther, all the consultants in this book, and I are more than happy to help you along this journey. Feel free to reach out to any of us at any time. We look forward to hearing from you, enjoy!

David Bitton
Co-Founder & CEO, PracticePanther
Miami, Florida
February 2018

THE FUTURE OF LEGAL TECH

By Robert Ambrogi

—

Robert Ambrogi is a lawyer and legal journalist who has been writing and speaking about legal technology and the Internet for more than two decades. He writes the award-winning blog LawSites, is a columnist for Above the Law, and cohosts the longest-running legal podcast, Lawyer2Lawyer, as well as the podcast Law Technology Now.

FOREWORD

The Future of Legal Tech

By Robert Ambrogi, *Founder, LawSitesBlog.com*

The year I first opened a solo practice, the Internet was not yet a thing. The PC had just come out and hardly any lawyer had one. Research was still done in libraries. "Marketing" meant attending lunches and local meetings. "Practice management" was done with a Rolodex, spiral-bound calendars, and lots of file folders.

The tools with which we practice law have changed dramatically since then. The Web has expanded our reach as lawyers, giving us access to new markets and vast resources. The cloud has provided us with easy access to powerful tools. And innovative companies such as PracticePanther have simplified the job of building and managing our practices and automated the chore of getting paid.

From a technology perspective, we are in a time of unprecedented innovation. It sometimes seems as though new legal startups appear every day. Artificial intelligence promises to greatly simplify our work. Legal analytics promise to predict case timelines and outcomes. Chatbots interface directly with clients.

However, for all this innovation, for all the ways technology has changed the legal landscape, the actual practice of law has not changed all that much from when I first started out. In their day-to-day practices, lawyers still struggle to balance the multiple tasks that face them – managing staff, keeping the books, marketing and business development, continuing education – it is amazing that lawyers find any time in the day to actually practice law.

The truth is that, for all the innovative tools available to us, lawyers have been slow to adopt and implement them. There are any number of reasons for this. Many lawyers still fear technology, or they simply do not understand it. It takes time to learn about new technologies and the best practices for using them – and time is something lawyers never have in surplus.

That is why a book such as this is so valuable. PracticePanther's CEO David Bitton has compiled contributions from many of the most-respected authorities in law practice management, marketing, and technology. They do the work for you, offering expert instruction in how to more effectively build, market, and manage your practice.

The tools are available to all of us. The secret to success is in knowing how to use them. This book gives you a big head start.

About Robert J. Ambrogi, Esq.

Robert Ambrogi is a lawyer and legal journalist who has been writing and speaking about legal technology and the Internet for more than two decades. He writes the award-winning blog LawSites, is a columnist for Above the Law, and cohosts the longest-running legal podcast, Lawyer2Lawyer, as well as the podcast Law Technology Now.

In 2011, Bob was named in the inaugural Fastcase 50, honoring "the law's smartest, most courageous innovators, techies, visionaries and leaders." In 2017, he received the Yankee Quill award for journalism from the Academy of New England Journalists and was honored by the ABA Journal as a Legal Rebels Trailblazer.

Earlier in his career, he was editor-in-chief of The National Law Journal and editorial director of ALM's Litigation Services Division. A 1980 graduate of Boston College Law School, he is a fellow of the College of Law Practice Management and immediate past-president of the Massachusetts Bar Foundation.

—

A HOW-TO GUIDE TO BUILDING A FIRM FROM THE BOTTOM UP

THE ULTIMATE CHECKLIST FOR STARTING YOUR OWN FIRM

By David Bitton

—

As an author, CLE speaker, and founder of PracticePanther.com, David is dedicated to automating law firms with the help of today's technology. He's revolutionizing the legal industry by helping lawyers get more done in less time using PracticePanther's practice management software.

CHAPTER 1

The Ultimate Checklist for Starting Your Own Firm

By David Bitton

Even if you already have your own firm, this chapter is still essential to help improve your website, get more leads, and enhance your brand. I recommend taking out a pen, and highlighting anything important to come back to later.

1. BUILD A WEBSITE

Having a great looking website is usually the first step in setting up your law firm online. You need to make a great first impression, and having a beautifully designed and functioning website is vital to your success.

Building a great looking site takes a considerable amount of time. If you have a lot of free time on your, I recommend reading through this first part. If you were thinking of building your website using Wix or Weebly or one of those DIY sites, the information below will help you get a better looking site. If however, you want the best website possible, you have money to spend, and your time is more valuable than building a site yourself, I recommend hiring a professional company that can do it for you, and jumping ahead to the second section to "Get More Traffic to Your Site."

If you're up for the challenge, the first step is to buy a domain name through GoDaddy.com. You want to keep the name short and simple. Try not to use any hyphens, and definitely only buy a domain name ending in .com and not some other variation like .org or .lawyer, it will only make it harder for people to remember. You want to register as a Private domain, instead of public. This hides your personal information like your home address, phone number, and other sensitive information, from the public search engines. A private domain name should cost you around $25/year, however, there are always coupon codes on Google that give you the first year for under $5 most of the time. Just go to Google and search for, "GoDaddy coupon codes." GoDaddy will try to upsell you on many additional services you really don't need, so skip through them and check-out.

The next step is to find a great template for your website. You only want to use a WordPress template. WordPress is a content management system (CMS), that allows you to easily add new pages, edit existing pages, have a blog, and look and feel like Microsoft Word's toolbar when editing the page. It's by far the number one most popular platform worldwide for building websites. You can take a look at PracticePanther.com as it's built on WordPress. My personal favorite place to find great looking WordPress templates is on ThemeForest.net. Click on the WordPress link on the top left to see all the options. I usually use the filters to sort by best sellers. Two of the top WordPress themes of all time are Avada and Enfold. They are one of the most customizable themes that many WordPress developers know how to work with easily. It may be hard to visualize how your site will look, so I recommend clicking on the theme, and seeing the difference options and layouts you can choose from. Keep in mind, everything is fully customizable. For example, if you look at the PracticePanther website, you would have never guessed it was built on Enfold because of how much customization we did over the years. Once you decided on your theme, go ahead and purchase it.

The next step is to create a Microsoft Word document with all the text and images you want on your website. You will give this information to your WordPress developer in the next step. The Word doc should have the list of pages on your site that you want to build. For example, the homepage, about the firm, practice areas, individual pages for each practice area, testimonials, case studies, a blog, FAQ, and a contact page. When planning this out, keep the flow of your site in mind. You want to design your site so you guide your viewers to the pages you want them to see first, second, third, etc. Finally, at the bottom of your site, you should have two buttons: the first is for people who are ready to make an appointment, and the second is for those who need more information.

You want to write exactly what text you want on each of those pages, along with the images for each page. If you don't have any images of yourself or your staff, now is the time to start taking them. No need to get fancy here, you can take them with your phone on a blank wall, or go to a photo studio and get a professional one for under $100.

As for design ideas, I strongly suggest you visit every website you love, including your competitors, and figure out what parts of the site you like. Maybe they have a large video at the top of their homepage, or a live chat feature. Feel free to add all of these ideas to your Word doc with links to reference what you mean. If you give your developer ideas with links, they will be able to help you achieve the exact same look, feel, and function of other sites you love. If you need help finding professional images or stock photos, you can search Google for "royalty-free stock photos" that you can download, or purchase for a minimal cost.

Once you have your pages mapped out, the content written, and the images selected, it's time to hire your WordPress developer to install the theme, and add your content in. You can find a WordPress expert, or really any expert in almost anything you can imagine, by going to UpWork.com. A lot of people will be talking about UpWork in this book, so it's a great time to start getting familiar with it. UpWork is one of the largest websites for finding talented freelancers worldwide. To get started, you should create a free account, and use the search bar to search for a "WordPress Developer." Use the filters to narrow the results even more. I like to select the following filters:

- English level: Fluent or Native
- Earned Amount: $10K+ earned
- Job Success: 90% & up
- Hourly Rate: $10 and below
- Hours Billed: 1,000+

- Last Activity: Within 2 weeks
- Freelancer Type: Independent
- Tests: WordPress (Scored in the top 10%)

As of this writing, these filters returned 63 of the top WordPress developers. So how do you choose the right one? I normally look for the ones that have a 97% to 100% Job Success rating. These are the ones that do everything in their power to make sure you are happy, and finish the job on time. After that, I look at the main title of their profile (listed in bold near their name). I look for titles that say something like, "WordPress Expert Developer & Designer." You want to find someone that has those words in their title, especially the word designer. This should narrow your results down to less than 10 people.

Now is the fun part. It's time to post your job, and invite your favorite freelancers to apply. On the top of UpWork, click on Jobs, and then Post a Job. The job title can be "WordPress theme & content installation". You want to post a job in the category of "WordPress Theme Development".

The description of the job post can say:
"Hi! We are excited to find a talented developer who can help build a WordPress site and maintain it for months to come. We need your help installing WordPress on our website, installing the theme we purchased, and placing all the text and images on the site. We also need your help with minor color changes, theme customization, installing WordPress plugins like Google Analytics. We would like you to help us verify our website with Google Webmaster tools, and install the robots.txt file to allow search engines to find our site. Please do not apply to this job if you cannot meet our budget constraints of $350 total. Please submit your most recent portfolio."

UpWork will ask you what skills the developer should have. You want to type in, "WordPress, Adobe Photoshop, CSS, HTML5, web-design, and SEO." You would like to pay a fixed price with a budget of $350. The estimated end date should be 3 weeks from your start date. Attach your document with your content so they can see what needs to get done. For preferred qualifications, the freelancer type should be no preference, minimum feedback score should be at least 4.5, hours billed should be at least 1,000. You should not have to pay more than $350 for a high quality WordPress website using a template (I know, shocking, isn't it?!).

Once you posted your job, go back to the top developers you liked, click on their profiles, and invite them to the job. Wait 24 hours, and see which ones replied back the fastest. This is usually a good indicator of who is readily available to get started right away. When you found the right one, hire them. UpWork will protect you by putting the money in escrow until the job is completed to your satisfaction, and you agree to end the job and release the funds.

You will need to provide your freelancer with the username and password of where you purchased your website (i.e. GoDaddy). Send them the theme you purchased, along with the Word Doc and any accompanying images. Start having a conversation, and make sure to reply back as fast as possible. If they have to wait 24 hours every time you respond, you will prolong the job. I recommend following up with the developer every few days to put some pressure and see how things are going. For some reason, many freelancers like to do all the work one day before the deadline. Once they submit the first draft, you will need to give them revisions. Feel free to give them as many revisions as needed until you are 100% happy. Keep in mind however, that if you keep adding more work, or new pages, it will cost more, so be upfront in the beginning with everything needed. The most important part is to be as responsive as possible, and you should have a new website in under 3 weeks.

I have a weird obsession with ripping through my friends websites and giving them advice on what to fix. If you end up building your website this way, I would love to give you feedback too. Feel free to email me at dbitton@practicepanther. com and expect a long reply with suggestions to send your freelancer.

2. GET MORE TRAFFIC TO YOUR SITE

There are some simple and quick things you can do to organically increase the traffic on your website.

If you search Google for any local businesses, you will usually see some results at the top of the page, with a map, and the names of 3 or more businesses. You will also see the number of star ratings each has. Generally, consumers will choose the business with the most reviews, and the highest rating. You want your business to be on this list. All you need to do is create a Google Business profile to get your firm listed in the Google Maps results. You can go to Google.com/business to claim your listing and setup your profile. They will send you a postcard to verify your address, and within 2 weeks you should have a Google Business listing. Remember, reviews will move up your listing and get you more clicks, so ask your current and past clients – those you know were happy with your work – to submit a nice, honest review. I generally see that it takes around 6 months to get to the top 3 results, so patience is key. You want to make sure you have more reviews than the current top 3 law firms. You also want to create the best possible listing which includes detailed descriptions, and as many photos as possible.

The next step to getting more traffic is to create a free listing in online directories like Avvo or FindLaw. The strategy is similar to Google Business - the more reviews you have, the higher on the list you will be placed. Furthermore, you can pay for their premium services so that you will be featured on the top of their directory and on Google searches. When someone is searching Google for "personal injury attorney in Miami" for example, they will generally find a directory like Avvo that will list all of these attorneys. You want to make sure you're on the very top of that list, with as many reviews as possible, as well as being at the top of every other list in the top 10 results of Google. When a consumer consistently finds your firm in the top results of every page, it will help influence their decision to contact you.

As you probably noticed, whenever searching for anything in Google, you will find many articles that match what you were searching for. Google is really good at showing results closely related to your search term and location. When you're blogging and adding articles to your website, you want to add your location into the title of your blog posts. If you're blogging about "How to find a personal injury attorney", you really want to call the blog post, "How to find a personal injury attorney in Miami, Florida." This way, Google will show your blog posts to people in your area. The common theme here is location. Just make sure you're writing blog posts that people are actually searching for, and are relevant to your law firm.

3. GET MORE LEADS FROM YOUR SITE

Now that you're generating more traffic to your site, you need to start getting more people to contact you. If you get 100 visits a month, but only 1 person contacts you, that's only a 1% conversion rate. What if you had a 10% conversion rate, can you imagine the amount of new business pouring through your door?

The good news is, it's not too hard to increase the conversion rating by following a few simple steps:

- Think of all the people who visit your site, but never call or email you. How come they didn't contact you? What questions did they have that they didn't ask? When you add a live chat feature to your site, it gives someone the opportunity to anonymously ask these questions, and start a conversation with you. We recommend using Zopim or Intercom, but there are plenty of other great options. You can have it automatically send a message after 5 seconds to every visitor asking, "Do you have any questions we can help with?" When the visitor responds, the message can be sent to your phone and computer, and you can respond right away. If you're not available, it can automatically follow up asking to give you their email address so you can reply later. The goal here is to start a conversation and capture their email address. You will have significantly more interaction when you install a live chat.

- It amazes me how hard it is to find a phone number on many attorneys websites. Your phone number should be prominently placed at the very top of every page on your site (called the header). It should be easy for people to know how to contact you. The number should also be clickable, so people on mobile devices can contact you instantly. What's even more amazing is how few law firms answer their phones. If a consumer can't reach you right away, they're moving on to the next listing on Google. Don't spend all this time and energy getting more traffic to your site, if you don't have a good system in place to answer every phone call by the 3rd ring. We'll speak more about this in future chapters on how you can automate this using tools like CallRuby.

• Consumers love to work with people they like and can relate to. If they like you, and they trust you, then they have a greater chance of becoming your client. So how do you become more personable without meeting or speaking to them? By using videos! Video marketing is an extremely effective way to show them who you and your firm is, what you stand for, why they should hire you. It also gives you an opportunity to answer any frequently asked questions they may have. I would love to give you a list of equipment here, but it will most likely be outdated in a few months, If you want, send me an email (dbitton@practicepanther.com) and I'll send you the latest tools, equipment, and procedures we use at PracticePanther to make our high quality videos. The amazing thing is, you can get away with recording great videos for under $100, or super professional videos for under $1,000, all by yourself.

4. THREE THINGS YOU DON'T WANT TO DO WRONG ON YOUR SITE

- In order to get more traffic to your site, everyone will tell you to do SEO (search engine optimization). This basically means you need to optimize your website so the search engines, mostly Google, can show your website to more people based on the keywords, search terms, and location they're searching for. One of the easiest ways to optimize your website is by making sure certain parts of your site have your law firm name, your main practice area, and your location. Instead of the title of your website being "Bitton Law", it should say, "Bitton Law | Personal Injury Attorney in Miami, FL." Once again, adding your location will give you a better ranking in the local, organic search results in Google. That way, people in Miami looking for a personal injury attorney will most likely find you. On the very bottom of every page on your website, called the footer, add the same title. It's all about keeping the same phrase or title consistent throughout your site.

- When you visit most websites, you're not really sure what to click on first. As stated previously, you want to direct your visitors to what you want them to view first, second, third, fourth, etc. Yes, you may need to actually spend a few minutes planning out the flow of your website, but trust me, it's well worth it. You do not want people to wander around or be confused. After they view the homepage, what should be the very next thing or page you want them to go to? For example, you may want them to visit your page on practice areas. Then, you can send them to your testimonials page. And finally, you can send them to your contact page. In the end, you always want people to contact you by either calling, emailing, or chatting with you online.

- In order to guide people throughout your site, you need what's called a "call to action" (CTA) button or link. Usually you want these buttons or links at the top and bottom of every page on your site. You want to end every page with the next step or action item your visitors should take. At the very bottom of every page on your site, you want to tell people what to do next with a button that will direct them through your website. These buttons should all lead to your contact page. You can also add a contact box on the bottom of every page to push them to contact you at any point during their search. The button on top of your site can say "View Practice Areas" and the button at the bottom of every page can say "Contact Us" for example. Keep in mind, the more buttons and options you add, the less likely they will know what to click on. I recommend reading "Don't Make Me Think" by Steve Krug. You don't want people to think when they're on your site. You want the next action button to be so simple, there is no other choice but to contact you. When you take them to your contact page, you generally have two options. You can keep these boxes simple and only ask for an email address if you want the most people to submit their information, or you can have a longer form if you want to pre-qualify people more, but get less messages. Either way, start implementing these changes today, and you'll likely see results instantly.

5. DESIGN A LOGO FOR UNDER $99

A logo is very important to your branding process. It's easy to ask your friend or neighbor to help, but you generally want a good logo from the onset as it becomes a pain to change it later once you have your website, business cards, and stationery printed. You can use the website UpWork.com to post a job, find freelancers, and create a custom logo based on your specifications. You can usually get a good logo designer for under $99 here. My personal favorite website however, and a bit more expensive, is 99Designs.com. They have thousands of talented logo designers that will bid for your business. The process is pretty simple. You submit a logo design contest, choose a budget, and give as much information as possible to what you're looking for. Then, different designers will start sending you their rough draft designs and ideas. You narrow down the results, choosing your top designs and designers, and the process keeps moving to the next stage. Eventually you end up in the final stage of revisions, usually with 3 designers, and you pick the winning design you liked best. The entire process takes around 7 days, and you're almost always guaranteed to get a design you'll be happy with. If not, you can ask for a time extension to get even more designs. The best part is, you will get so many different designers who will provide so many different designs and ideas, and it's very exciting to see all the creativity of what your logo can become. By the way, this is how we designed PracticePanther's logo.

6. DESIGN YOUR OWN BUSINESS CARDS

A good business card can convey your level of professionalism and your brand. However, even a good-looking card that isn't printed properly will lose its effect. The worst thing you can do is hand someone a business card that says, "Printed for free from Vistaprint.com". There are many websites that will create custom card designs for you (UpWork.com), or, you can buy DIY templates (GraphicRiver.net). You can also use 99Designs.com to get a custom designed card. Once you have the design, the next step is printing. I highly recommend spending a little extra, but getting a thicker, nicer, better quality card. My favorite website is Moo.com because of their ease of use, support, and card quality. If you're working with a business card designer, you want them to know you plan on working with Moo.com so they can design the card with the exact same specs that Moo requires. If you really want to splurge, go with the Luxe cards from Moo. It's one of the thickest and heaviest business cards you can buy. I always love the reaction when people think I gave them two cards because of the paper weight.

7. CREATE YOUR OWN EMAIL CAMPAIGN

An attractive email campaign can demonstrate to clients your professionalism and keep you on their mind. It is actually quite easy to create a beautiful email campaign once you follow these steps:

1. Go to GraphicRiver.net and find a predesigned email campaign template. You can use the search box and type in the word "MailChimp",

since this is the company you will use to send out your emails. Most designs are under $10. Once you find a design you like, purchase it.

2. Go to MailChimp.com, create a free account and use the "Automation" feature. If the automation feature isn't on the free plan anymore, it's worth the extra cost. This feature will automatically send email campaigns to new and current clients in your list on auto-pilot.

3. Before you send your first email campaign out, you need to edit the template, and place it into MailChimp. Instead of doing it yourself, you want to hire a MailChimp expert from UpWork.com. I recommend searching for a designer by typing in "PSD to MailChimp" into the search box. Follow the same steps as mentioned earlier in the book to filter the results and find the best freelancer. By the way, PSD is a Photoshop design file. You want to find an expert that can take the PSD template you purchased, and convert it to a beautiful looking email template in MailChimp that you will be able to use forever. Once you hire the freelancer, tell them exactly how you want the template to look, and give them all the content and images to include.

4. Once you approve of their design, ask them to put the template into MailChimp for you, and show you how to set it up and start sending.

5. Once you've setup your first email campaign, clone the custom template and change the content around so you create at least five different email campaigns. You can use the automation feature to automatically send an email to every person you add to your list. The goal is to send 1 email out every month or quarter so your current and past clients continue to hear from you. When it's time for them to hire or refer a lawyer, they should hopefully think of you right away thanks to your email campaigns.

8. GET A FREE BUSINESS PHONE NUMBER

It is easy to make and receive calls to your cell phone using a different number. You can sign up for a free number on Google.com/voice. Calls to that number will be forwarded to your phone or any other phone you choose. Caller ID will show whether the call is a personal or business call, so you can adjust your demeanor accordingly. For example, when you see a call coming in from Google Voice, you can answer differently by saying, "Thank you for calling the law offices of Smith and Cohen, how can I help you?" My favorite part – you can even get missed calls sent to your email inbox when you cannot answer, your phone doesn't have service, or is turned off.

Voicemails are also transcribed to text and emailed to you as an MP3. Google Voice also provides an automatic spam filter to reduce the number of spam calls you get. You can even link your credit card to Google Voice so you can make extremely affordable international calls at rates similar to Skype or any other VOIP provider.

9. GET A PROFESSIONAL 800 NUMBER

It is important for your branding to have an 800 number. This makes you look more professional, and almost like a nationwide law firm. 800 numbers can forward all calls to your cell phone, as well as call out using an 800 number. In the past I've used both Phone.com and RingCentral.com, and they offer similar features and pricing. New customers can usually receive half off with a coupon code you can find online.

You can set up a directory to forward calls to specific people or add extensions. Set up office hours and after hours with a custom voicemail for each. Fiverr.com offers voicemails recorded by a professional voiceover artist.

10. LOOK BIGGER WITH A VIRTUAL RECEPTIONIST

As I said before, all this work will go to waste if you don't answer your phone when a new client calls. A virtual receptionist can make your firm appear bigger than it really is, and help you answer every call within seconds. When you have a professional secretary or receptionist answering every call, your clients feel that they can always reach you at any time of day. The best part is, you don't even need an office to have a live receptionist. Virtual receptionists are trained to answer calls professionally, and with your exact welcome script. A service we highly recommend is CallRuby.com – they were even kind enough to provide you with $75 off your first invoice by using the promo code PANTHERSOFTWARE.

11. HOW TO BLOG

There are two goals for blogging:
1. To seem like a knowledgeable, trustworthy professional.
2. To get people to find your post, come to your site, look around your site, and eventually contact / hire you.

The first step in blogging is to make a list of topics to write about. They should be things people are searching for. How exactly do you know what people are searching for, though? A really easy way is to start typing something into Google, and you will see suggested search results. This usually is a good indicator of what other people are searching for. You can also scroll down to the bottom of Google's search results, and it will show you related searches with more ideas you can use. Each related option could be another subheading or paragraph in your blog post. An easier way to get your post to the top of Google is to make sure it has a good "long-tail" keyword, as we call it. Instead of blogging about "Questions to ask a lawyer," you should blog about "10 Questions to ask a family law attorney in Miami, Florida before hiring them." Many experts in this book, including myself, will only recommend one platform for blogging: WordPress. Within minutes, you, or an expert, can help install WordPress on your website, and you can be blogging in no time.

Here are some general tips as to where the title of your blog post should appear:
1. In the title of the blog post itself, of course.
2. In the URL and link of the blog post. When you save your first post as a draft, WordPress will show you the link of where it will be. Instead of having your link be www.smithcohenlawmiami.com/post-32, it should say www.smithcohenlawmiami.com/10-questions-ask-family-lawyer-miami-florida.
3. In the actual blog post as a HEADER 1. When you're writing your post, you can change the size of the text. Make one title or header be in the H1 font size. Why do we do this? So Google's robots see it as the largest font on the page, and understand it's the most important.

Blog posts should be a minimum of 400 words. The most shared posts apparently are in the 1,600-2,000 word range these days, but don't go crazy if you can't get there. We like to aim for standard blog posts around 750 words, which tend to work quite well for us.

Remember to use eye-catching images. There are plenty of ways to find royalty-free and stock photos online for no charge. You can either download and use them for free, or, pay a website like ShutterStock.com for high quality premium images. Another bonus tip – before you upload the image to WordPress, rename the file on your computer to the same name as the title of your post. When someone searches Google Images, the image will come up in the search results bringing you some extra free traffic.

It is also extremely important to link to other articles or pages on your site. Google's robots love when you do this. It also helps people continue browsing your site for longer, showing Google that your site has relevant high-quality content that keeps people on your site for longer than usual. This is one of the reasons Facebook is so valuable, because the average human spends insane amounts of time daily on their platform.

I'm saving my best tip for last. Do yourself a favor and download and install the WordPress SEO Plugin by Yoast to your WordPress site. When you write your next WordPress post or page, scroll to the bottom, and you will see a section titled "Yoast SEO." This is where it will show you how the post or page will look in Google. It will also give you an analysis and let you know how many times your main keyword was used on the page, if your title is too short, and a number of other action items to check. It also has advanced settings that will help get your website, blog, posts, and pages picked up by Google.

I really hope you go back through this chapter and write down some actionable steps to take in the next 24 hours to improve your website, build a great brand, and grow your firm. I know I may have oversimplified many of these steps, so please feel free to reach out if you have any questions, or want me to critique your website. Send an email to **dbitton@practicepanther.com** and I'll be more than happy to help.

EIGHT (WELL, REALLY 33) TIPS FOR STARTING YOUR OWN LAW FIRM

By Barbara Leach

Barbara J. Leach is the managing attorney of Barbara Leach Law, PL whose office is located in the heart of Orlando. Her firm concentrates on representing individuals and small businesses, helping them with family and bankruptcy issues and other litigation dilemmas.

CHAPTER 2

Eight (well, really 33) Tips for Starting Your Own Law Firm

By Barbara Leach

Babs here, and if you're reading this, congratulations! You've taken the first (or maybe 50th) step on the way to owning your own law firm. Few things are more thrilling – or scarier – than taking that leap, but throughout this chapter, I prefer to focus on the more thrilling components of this undertaking. So, again, I say, congrats!

I opened my own law firm in 2011 without clients and about $400 worth of assets - namely a printer, laptop, and $100 worth of office supplies, because I have an office supply fixation. I have many suggestions for you, but have categorized them into eight sections. Of course, I'm biased enough to think there is value in all of them, regardless of your practice area.

1. ROW UP YOUR DUCKS

Let's start with some of the backroom, non-sexy stuff. I cannot stress enough the importance of having an email address that does not end in yahoo.com or gmail.com. In these days, it is super easy and relatively inexpensive to (a) purchase a domain name, and (b) set up your own email address at that URL. For instance, I have www.bleachlaw.com, and our office emails are consistently people's first names: barbara@bleachlaw.com. I pay about $10.00 a month for Microsoft 365 to host my email, and I assure you, that is money well spent.

Think of it this way: your potential clients and referrals are not going to take you seriously if your email them something like barbara.jean.leach@gmail.com or bleachlawoffice@yahoo.com. We discuss below the importance of branding, but for now, remember, most people do not know the qualities that make up a good lawyer, so they're looking for outward signs that might be an indication of your success. If you're successful, then you must be good at what you do, right? I believe there have been many Ponzi schemes established on this basic tenet. Obviously, that's not our goal here, but you get the picture. So, invest in an email address with a proper domain name before you go a step further!

Even before you select a URL, establish a "kitchen cabinet" or "advisory board" of trusted friends/colleagues/business gurus so you can run ideas by them. Before deciding on bleachlaw.com, I had about four other ideas I was playing with (most of them bad ideas, according to my group of advisors that I like to call my "Rectangle"). This group of trusted advisors consists of three of my closest friends: Melanie Griffin, Jacquelynne Regan, and Jessica McGinnis. With the Rectangle's encouragement, I selected bleachlaw.com. Having engaged in protracted conversations with them and getting unfiltered feedback, I felt comfortable in my decision to go with that one. That comfort immediately translated into a feeling of confidence that I had made the right decision, because it wasn't only MY decision, but the decision of a group.

The next step is to figure out an office address and phone number. More on that below, as it relates to selecting an office (spoiler alert: do you even need an office?). Obviously, you should have a mailing address and phone number before you incorporate your firm. Make sure to also get your city, county, and state licenses to operate your business. In Central Florida for example, you need a license for both your business and yourself as an attorney. There might be similar quirks in your backyard, so take time to research thoroughly at the onset. You are a lawyer, after all!

After setting up your mailing address and license(s), which serve to validate your physical footprint, it's time to go online and establish your virtual footprints. By this I mean it's important to create a Facebook Business page, an Instagram account, Snapchat, LinkedIn, Pinterest, Twitter, YouTube Channel, and any other social media platform that exists at the time you are reading this.

Hold on. I know. It's as though I can hear your thoughts radiating through the pages: "But Babs, wait, I don't have those in my personal life - why would I ever need a Pinterest account for my law firm?" I'm not here to suggest you need, or even want, any of these. The goals are to claim them in the event you change your mind and to prevent others from claiming them!

The key throughout this process is this: wherever you can, consistently use the same name, nickname, and handle. This is a case of "do as I say, not as I do." Right now, I have an identity crisis on Twitter. I am bleachlaw, pinkladylawyer, babsybikes, and barbarajeanleach (I think). I don't tweet at all, but I am ready! I also have chilawhua and babsbakesbliss on Instagram. One of them is to stalk cookie bakers, and the other is to post about my cookie obsession. But back to the importance of consistency - you are establishing your brand, and you want to make it easy for clients and referral sources to identify and locate you.

While you're at it, go ahead and claim your Avvo profile. Yes, I know, there are a ton of anti-Avvo lawyers. But at the end of the day, Avvo isn't going away, consumers use it consistently to locate and vet attorneys they ultimately hire, and Mark Britton, its founder and CEO, is a swell fellow who is seeking to do good in this world. So, stop trying to swim upstream, embrace the Avvo, and have it work for you. Go ahead and plant your flag on a Google+ profile too.

As I mentioned, I started my law practice with a laptop, printer, and about sixty-five pounds of multi-colored Post-its. My next two big investments were a logo and my malpractice insurance. I am certain I paid over $1,000.00 for each (way more than I should have paid for the logo - did I mention the subtitle of this chapter is "Learn from my Mistakes?") Depending on what state you are in, malpractice insurance might be optional. It is in Florida. Even though I wasn't required to have insurance, I got it for peace of mind. Opening your own law firm shakes your confidence to the core. "Is this the right thing? Will someone hire me? Will I ever get a paycheck? Am I competent? Am I going to go crazy with no one to talk to? Am I going to get sued?" You second-guess EVERY decision, and you get worried that something like the color of your logo might run off potential clients (speaking from experience, folks, don't judge). So, whatever you can do to instill confidence in yourself will pay tremendous dividends. This directly translates to a confidence portrayed to potential clients, who then feel more secure in hiring a lawyer whose office paint hasn't even dried. For me, knowing that I had insurance to cover any potential screw-ups allowed me to breathe easier.

2. CREATE SYSTEMS

One of my greatest joys in life is to create order out of chaos, and I suspect that's true for all lawyers. So right now, this is your chance to create order BEFORE there's chaos. In the event one of your first reactions to starting your own firm wasn't, "Oh boy! Now I get to create procedures!" I suggest you read The *E-Myth Attorney*, or, The *E-Myth Revisited*, both by Michael Gerber. The former is specific to lawyers, the latter more general, but both have value. The concept behind *The E-Myth* is that every practice should be based on a series of specific, delineated steps for every role, task, and procedure within a law firm.

"But Babs, it's just me. I don't have any staff. Heck, I don't even have any clients yet! Why do I need written procedures on how to answer the phone?!" I hear you, I hear you. But I encourage you to embrace the Stephen Covey philosophy to "Begin with the end in mind." Sure, right now you don't have staff or associate attorneys working with you, but there's a great likelihood that will change in the near future. Usually, you bring on new team members when you really need them. And by "really need them," I mean that you are going to be so busy that you will need to hire quickly, and the last thing you have is time to train them as properly as they deserve to be trained. Enter: a procedures binder.

Within the first month of me deciding I was going to start my own firm, I remember sitting up in bed, pillows tucked behind my back, yellow legal pad in my lap, carefully and thoughtfully crafting the "How to open a new client file" tab that would be the first of many process outlines to adorn my procedures binder. I chuckled aloud, asking Brulee the ChiLAWhua (my long-haired Chihuahua sidekick), "How funny is THIS? We don't have any clients, and the only person to use this procedure is going to be the person who creates it?"

But I had a vision. One day I would hire someone who would go through these specific steps, and I wanted consistency and accuracy for every step of these processes.

"But Babs, my practice is so specialized I will never have another person working with me. Surely I don't need procedures?" Yes, you do, and don't call me Shirley. Seriously, I respect that "But Babs," but let me suggest this: Another benefit to sitting down and thoughtfully, carefully thinking through each procedure is that when you take the time to write out steps to accomplish a task, it allows you to identify flaws in your process. I am a huge proponent of efficiency, and I believe taking the time to analyze each step in a process equips you to accomplish the process more efficiently.

If this isn't enough to convince you of the value of establishing a process for everything – including how to label file folders – then I encourage you to read *The Checklist Manifesto* by Atul Gawande. He articulates the efficacy of a system much more so than I. If you chuckled over the absurdity of time spent crafting a procedure to label file folders, I will confess that is one of the procedures I have developed. I will further confess that I spent an hour drafting that. But in the six years since I created that procedure, not a single intern, law clerk, receptionist, paralegal, or assistant has ever asked me how to label a file folder. So, balance one hour versus repetitive instruction, and I think you'll see one hour was time well spent. All of this is actually kind of old-school now, because most of my files are paperless, but still…

3. EMBRACE TECHNOLOGY

I'm not sure where on our law school diplomas or our bar passage certificates it is hidden, but somewhere in invisible ink are the words, "I will endeavor to be a Luddite." Most of us fear technology or exist in a state of technological denial, refusing to believe that technology is anything other than a hindrance. That philosophy could not be further from the truth. When you are starting your firm, that is the time when it is easiest to embrace technology in order to make your life easier, more efficient, and revenue-generating. The first place to start is practice management software.

This is one of those "teaching moments" (again, otherwise known as the "do as I say, not as I…" I can't even finish that sentence for the shame of it). I didn't have a practice management software program until I'd had my firm for two years. I thought, "It's just me; I can't afford it; Excel and Word are good enough; I can keep track of my billing without it" and a host of other well-intentioned ideas.

By waiting two years to adopt practice management, it actually cost me more in the long run. More specifically, I had to pay someone to set up client files for both current and closed matters and input/import over 200 cases worth of data. This actually cost me overtime wages because, by the time I came to this realization, I was knee-deep in the middle of running a law practice. It was horribly inefficient, in addition to costly, because I didn't have the luxury of extra time to learn how to input billable hours, run reports, and sort through data. I needed to be fully up-to-speed and functioning at a 100% understanding. Instead, I paid for extra help and spent extra hours trying to get a handle on this software while juggling my cases. I don't even want to think about the money I left on the table because of all the time I didn't capture.

People regularly ask me, "What's the one thing you'd change?" or "What is the one thing you regret?" The answer is quick and easy: "I wish I had a practice management software from the outset." Again, when you begin with the end in mind, you realize you have to plan for a mechanism by which to capture time, create bills, accept payments, house correspondence and communication, create and delegate tasks, generate checklists, and generate productivity reports. While all of these things are achievable with a typewriter and an abacus, why waste valuable time (which translates directly to money) when there's a way to do it efficiently and relatively inexpensively?

"But Babs, of course you're saying that; this is a chapter in a book put together by a practice management software company." True, but for better or worse, I assure you my thoughts are my own! And this is something I'm passionate about. Again, learn from my mistakes.

There is a myriad of options out there: server based, cloud based, buy the whole system, or monthly subscriptions. I suggest three things:

1. Talk to your colleagues. I highly recommend speaking to the ones that are already solo practitioners, as they've already gone through these decisions.
2. Talk to the professionals. Take ten minutes and identify what you need practice management to do for you, then speak to the various program reps about what services they provide.
3. And if you sign up for a trial period on a program, USE IT. Don't attempt to delegate this to your husband, your "tech-savvy" teenager, or your paralegal who will be the one using the software the most. That's another mistake I made: when I was first trying to figure out what to use, I delegated that to a couple of law clerks. They came up with a brilliant analysis and a thoughtful comparison, neither of which amounted to a hill of beans because they couldn't really anticipate what was important to me, my firm's needs, or my firm's future goals.

Just suck it up and put it on your calendar to spend at least ten hours over a three-week period kicking the tires on a variety of systems. Just like the time initially invested in creating "How to Label a File Folder," I assure you, time spent figuring out and money invested on a system that works for you will pay off almost immediately. "But Babs, I'm spending all this other time coming up with these systems—when do I start making money?" Soon, trust me. Maybe you're not going to bring in wheelbarrows of cash while you're spending time trying to figure out which practice management system has the best support, but if you're just opening your firm, you likely don't have a plethora of clients either. Get in the habit of working hard now, even if it isn't billable, and it will pay off.

And speaking of investing time in non-billable undertakings, I highly suggest buying an iPad or some sort of tablet, attending at least one legal technology conference, and figuring out how to download copious apps on your smartphone, all dedicated to increasing your efficiency, portability, and productivity. Why? Time and money! If you engage in the sweat equity now to learn about how to make your practice the most efficient, there will be a payoff in terms of increased free time, or revenue, or maybe both if you're lucky!

Applications such as PDF Expert allow you to view and edit PDFs on an iPad. Each month, my paralegal forwards my prebills, and I review and edit them on my iPad. I used to print them out - over 200 pages of them - to go through each page and make notes, but now it's done on my iPad (oftentimes in a pedicure or hairdresser's chair).

Checklist Again, Todoist, and Wunderlist are wonderful checklists/todo list apps. There's a part of me that thinks Evernote is my own personal Google—any questions I need answered about my life can be found in my exhaustive Evernote files and notes.

This is just a smattering of apps that I use on a daily basis, but if you want to take a drink out of a legal technology firehose instead of standing by the water cooler, I suggest you attend the ABA TECHSHOW, occurring annually mid-March in Chicago. TECHSHOW is a three-day conference that brings together legal technology authorities, cutting-edge vendors, and savvy practitioners, all looking to teach and learn from each other. Take lots of notes, and when you get home, close your office door for a solid eight hours to absorb and implement what you've learned. Then, begin sharing these programs, apps, and gadgets with your friends who didn't attend TECHSHOW. Not only will you seem like the great and powerful Oz, but talking about these ideas actually forces you to implement them.

4. GET INVOLVED

When I first started practicing, a well-respected rainmaker told me that I needed to join at least three organizations: one legal professional organization, one community or philanthropic association, and one religious or political professional group. It should go without saying that one way to build your practice is to put yourself in front of people who need to hire lawyers or need to refer people to lawyers. I joined and then became President of the Central Florida Association for Women Lawyers, and I'm active in the Florida State Bar. I also volunteered with the Orlando Shakespeare Theater and the ALS Association.

A reminder: it's not enough to just "join." You have to get involved. I don't expect you to become president or chair of every organization you join, but it's important to do more than just show up for mediocre chicken lunches or stroke quarterly checks for good causes.

Even more specifically, I encourage you to be one of the first ones at a meeting and one of the last ones to leave. "But Babs, I barely have time to go to lunch, let alone go early and stay late. It will be a two-hour time commitment!" When I hear people lament over this suggestion, I remind them—if you are going to already be investing well over an hour to attend a lunch, you might as well take a deep breath and invest an extra twenty minutes. Most people are daunted by entering a large room full of people who are expecting to engage in small talk and make "meaningful" connections. What's the best way to avoid walking into a big group? Go when there are fewer people! This is your prime time to connect with people. It's really hard to do so when you're sitting at a table and are supposed to be quietly listening to a featured luncheon speaker.

While we're talking about networking, it shouldn't be your goal to hand out as many business cards as possible. Rather, your focus should be on collecting business cards. "But Babs, I want people to call me and send me clients!" I assure you, that is not likely to happen unless your first impression was both extraordinary, and that person had an exact need for the exact service you offer at the exact time you met them.

Typically, at networking functions, we gather business cards and do nothing with them, regardless of what we say we are going to do, i.e., "I will follow up with these people. I mean it." If you give out your cards, you don't get to control what happens next with the people you meet. That's not to say don't give out cards. Do so, but focus on getting them, and then as soon as you get back to your office – that day or the next – send each of those people a hand-written note card with your firm logo on it. In that card, let him/her know it was a pleasure meeting them, and you'd love to get together for coffee, lunch, or drinks. Then, calendar to follow up with them about a week later via email and get something on the books.

"But Babs, I'm just starting my firm; I don't have money to go to lunch or drinks or coffee all the time." I totally get that. And that's why it's important to be strategic about the meetings you schedule. Check out the calendar of your local bar and see if they have committees or sections based upon your interest or practices area. For example, I'm a member of these committees: technology, solo/small firm, family law, and bankruptcy. Don't forget to check when these committees meet. When I was starting out, I tried to attend as many brown bag lunches as possible, because I didn't need to spend as much money to attend those events. Further, I encourage you to schedule follow-up coffees as opposed to lunch dates. This saves you a tremendous amount of dough, and you can be a hotshot when you pay for your guest's hot (yet inexpensive) beverage.

While we're talking about collecting business cards and what to do with them, I cannot impress upon you enough the importance of creating contacts for all these people. I store everyone in Outlook, and that way, I can access it on any device, sync it to my telephone, and export and import depending upon where I'm working or what email provider is my host. Database managers talk about garbage in is garbage out, so it's important to create your contacts and keep them updated. I like to put a sentence in the notes section of each contact to remind me how I met them, or who they might also know. This is both a reminder of how we met and sometimes a trigger that in the event I can't remember someone by their name, I can remember what restaurant we met at or what area they practice.

"But Babs, I don't have time to go to lunch or out for drinks every day either. I spend enough time nurturing the clients and contacts I already have." My response is to read Keith Ferrazzi's book, Never Eat Alone. Ferrazzi is the master of establishing and nurturing relationships, and his book is full of concrete ways to facilitate this.

For that matter, who says these have to be one-on-one coffees? Why not introduce one of your financial planner friends to an accountant colleague and invite along a trust and estates lawyer also? Being the person who can connect others is an invaluable skill, and these casual coffee dates are the way you get good at it and known for it.

A good friend of mine, Ashley Winship (an amazing estate attorney), bi-annually hosts a happy hour with a couple of other non-lawyer colleagues, and they each handpick about seven professional friends. The whole purpose of this well-attended function is to meet new people, and specifically, potential referral sources. Ashley and her friends are rock stars in our eyes because we get to meet top-notch people at those events. What's to say you can't do that yourself? Start small. Host it at your office. It's a lot cheaper to buy a few bottles of mediocre wine, a case of beer, and some cheese and crackers at Costco than to rent out a private room in a fancy wine bar. Save that for when you're rolling in the dough. For now, trust me – your attendees care more about the guests than what food and drinks you're offering. Your energy and enthusiasm should totally outshine any fancy décor at a nice restaurant. Keep it simple; the emphasis is on your guests.

I like for my guests to leave my events with something to commemorate their time. Nowadays, since I'm obsessed with cookies. Invariably, part of a "goodie bag" is Babs Bakes, but that's only part of it. I'm a big fan of a printed item with my logo on it. When going through the process of starting your firm, it's important to start a relationship with a promotional products professional.

"But Babs, I can just Google that sort of thing." Absolutely true. But what I love about my professional, Heather at Blue Sky Promotions, is that I can say to her, "Heather, what's new and exciting for under $2.00?" She will give me several options, usually in under a day. Then she handles everything, and all I have to do is figure out how I'm going to package these goodies. As we will discuss later, it is important to delegate what you can, so you can focus on either bringing in the work or getting it done. Sure, I could spend a couple of hours tracking down the best place to buy Post-it notes, but I've saved maybe $40.00, and I've just lost two billable hours. So establish that relationship before you need it.

That happy hour for your professional colleagues can also be extended to an event or two for your clients. Annually, I host a Valentine's Party as a way to say (at the risk of sounding corny) "I love you" to my clients and my colleagues. Conti Moore of Conti Moore Law and I used to share an office, and we had a big bash every year. We hosted an open-house lunch from 11-2, and anyone could drop in during that three hours. The first year, we had 150 people attend. It was awesome. We hired a photo booth that gave out unlimited copies of pictures, and we had BBQ from the most popular joint in town. We didn't do a holiday party because everyone's calendars fill up over the holidays. So, we staked our claim on Valentine's Day.

When our lease was up and we got our own places, I changed the lunch to a Valentine's happy hour, and Conti started hosting a Mardi Gras party. This is great because we can go to each other's events and not dilute the other person's function's attendance. I encourage you to think about something you can do on an annual basis that could be a "signature" event. "But Babs, what if only ten people come?" That's awesome! Because you only have to worry about feeding ten people and will have tons of leftovers! But invite two hundred. By sending the invitation to people, you make them feel appreciated - even if they don't come. So, your objective is met, even with less than ten percent in attendance. Just make sure those ten people have the time of their lives, so they go back to their offices and tell everyone how awesome the party was and eagerly await the next one. Trust me, that ten will easily double the next year, maybe even quadruple! Just make sure I make it onto the invite list since it was my idea, ok?

5. CREATE YOUR BRAND FROM DAY ONE

I mentioned the importance of establishing a relationship with a promotional products professional and sending out notes on notecards with your logo. I also alluded to the fact that one of my largest investments up front was my logo. This was important to me because I wanted to establish my brand from the very beginning. Before I opened my office - before I hosted my law firm launch party - I had printed business cards, embossed letterhead and envelopes, and full-color notecards.

"But Babs why do I need to spend money on these things? I can get free business cards from Vistaprint, I can print my letterhead myself, and I can get cute notecards from Hallmark." Again, you're spot on. But ask yourself this: How much weight do you give to people who hand you flimsy business cards with the law firm name typed out in an italics font…as if italics makes lawyers more legit. Design your own logo if you happen to have a background in graphics arts; otherwise, go to a logo competition website like 99designs.com where you tell designers how much you're willing to pay for the winning design. Anywhere from twenty to two hundred designers will give you their best ideas, and before you know it, voila - you're on your way to being as brand-famous as Coca-Cola or FedEx.

My firm color is purple, so wherever I can, I incorporate a deep, rich purple into my marketing. Heck, I've been known to wear a purple suit when I'm presenting a CLE. I just love it when one matches their PowerPoint, don't you? And true confession: I actually own at least three purple suits…

I really wanted pink to be my firm color, because I'm girly and love pink. I didn't end up with pink because The Rectangle was afraid I would lose potential clients as people wouldn't take me seriously enough. So, the compromise was purple, but I have pink accents in my office. Lots of pink.

6. BE FRUGAL

You don't build a successful law firm by cutting down on expenses. You build it by increasing revenue. Having said that, though, for the first couple of years, you want to run as lean an operation as possible while you figure out what it takes to be successful.

Do you need Class A office space? Do you even need an office? When I first started, I had a shared workspace. I thought it was important for me to have someone answer my phones and have a street address, not a P.O. Box. I wanted access to a conference room where I could meet clients when I needed to. But remember, I started my practice with zero clients, so I suspected I wouldn't need a conference room right away. Turns out I was right. In fact, I think my first five clients hired me without meeting me in person. We talked on the phone, and then they hired me.

A shared workspace was perfect for me. I knew I needed a setup that would allow me to grow in the same location, as opposed to moving to a different address. I figured I would use a shared workspace for a year, and then I could rent an office from the same building. I also thought that by my second-year anniversary, I would be ready to hang my physical shingle in my own office space.

Things didn't quite go as planned. Those two years actually happened within nine months because my business grew so fast. Luckily, I had a plan, and I looked at potential offices with that time frame in mind. Since I figured I might be in three different office configurations within two years, I didn't want to be that lawyer who moved around a lot. When I visited shared workspace options, I made sure to ask questions about renting offices on a monthly basis and tour them before making my final decision.

Some shared workspace providers don't allow you to take the phone number they assign you when you leave their building. That was a deal breaker for me. I knew I'd change offices, perhaps many times in the course of my career, but I never wanted my phone number or email address to change. Today, I think the solution is to come up with your own number first and then forward it to the shared workspace office.

Once you're ready to take the leap to your own office, please don't spend a ton of money on fancy, new furniture. Check out used office furniture stores and Craigslist. Conti and I furnished our entire office from these resources, with the exception of our conference room table. And even that we negotiated a deal on. The only advice I have about going through Craigslist is: (a) be prepared to pull the trigger if you find something you like because good quality, reasonably priced office furniture goes quickly on Craigslist; and (b) establish a relationship with a mover. I'm not talking about a professional moving company that is used to moving entire offices. I'm talking about someone you can pick up the phone and say, "Lorenzo (our mover), can you go to Altamonte Springs on Thursday and pick up four desks and seven chairs?" And he does it.

I can't stress enough the importance of establishing relationships with professionals before you need them. I already know who will one day captain my yacht and fly my plane, even though I might be a bit further away from hiring them than I'd like to be!

7. SPEND SOME MONEY

We've already outlined a couple of instances where I think it's important to spend some money: investing in a good logo and high-quality business cards. We've also discussed the importance of delegating tasks when you can. At some point, you'll begin to see there are tasks that you can pay someone $20-$40 an hour to complete and free up your time in order for you to focus on the things only you can do, such as practice law and bring in clients.

We have discussed throwing happy hours at your office to bring together professional colleagues, and we even talked about how I do an annual Valentine's party and invite colleagues, clients, and friends, many of whom fall into all three categories! What we have not discussed was the big bash I threw when I opened my law firm, and I would encourage you to plan something similar.

When I decided to go out on my own, I planned a law firm launch party. I mailed out a physical invitation that was an announcement of my firm opening, and an invitation to celebrate with me. Remember how I said collecting Outlook Contacts was important? Well, I started that long before I owned my firm, and I had about 1,000 contacts to whom I wanted to mail my announcement and invite. I hired a law student to ensure all addresses were updated, a process she started about two months before I had my party because I figured it would take an ungodly amount of time. I was right.

I planned this party, catered it with the same BBQ I mentioned that everyone loves, and the dad of a friend of mine, Amanda Perry Carl, came and DJed for us. I had a signature drink, name tags, and goodie bags. Honestly, it was like planning a wedding for 225 people. At one point, when the party was really rocking, I stood in a corner with two of my prior bosses, simply observing the partygoers having a great time. I was overwhelmed by the energy and excitement in the room. And all of these folks were there to celebrate the start of my business.

I threw that party for two reasons: I wanted to celebrate my launch, and I wanted to let people know I was open for business. Looking back, I am certain that party was the reason why my firm has always (knock on wood) been profitable - after I bought that logo and malpractice insurance, that is. "But Babs, I don't have that many people to invite!" Just as I said above, it's ok if only ten people come. The idea is that you show those ten people an awesome time and how excited you are about your new law firm!

8. ADOPT A GIVING MENTALITY

We've talked a lot about you – ways for you to open your firm, ways for you to network to get clients, ways for you to save money, ways for you to spend money. Now let's talk about others. People are going to ask you for help. For example, "Do you know someone who practices mobile home repossession law?" or "Who do we know who can help a client object to a lien stripping in a bankruptcy case?" Believe me, inquiries about random, obscure practice areas will come your way. The easy answer is, "No" and go on with your day. But that doesn't help others.

I'm a firm believer that the way to succeed is to help others succeed. Take the time to refer the business to someone else, and you'll be surprised how many people will reciprocate.

The short of it is: help others. Gary Vaynerchuk's Jab, Jab, Jab, Right Hook is not a boxing primer; rather it's a book dedicated to the premise of give, give, give, ask. The idea is that people will be more willing to help you after you put some skin in the game by helping them. And the simplest way to do that is to try and answer questions they inevitably will ask you.

Another way we lawyers can adopt a jab-jab mentality is to educate people about our practice areas. Take me for example. I regularly talk to bankruptcy practitioners about family law issues involved in their cases, and I regularly explain bankruptcy implications to family law lawyers. Maybe I see a bankruptcy question posted on a Facebook lawyers group of which I'm a member or a family law question asked on a solo/small firm listserv. In those cases, I respond and say, "Hey, call me, and let's talk about this." Yes, that ends up being about fifteen minutes of my time, but I have done three things by that: (1) helped a colleague out, (2) demonstrated my subject-matter knowledge, and (3) further cemented our relationship.

All of this goes a long way to establishing a referral relationship. Ninety-five percent of my practice is referrals, and ninety percent of that is referrals from other lawyers. We've spent a long time emphasizing the importance of establishing relationships before you need them, right? Well, the same thing applies here. Let your colleagues establish that YOU are the go-to family law, or criminal defense, or commercial law, or trust and estates attorney, so when someone comes to them needing a referral, you are a no-brainer. After all, you've already demonstrated your knowledge of the subject, right? So, it's an easy choice to refer you.

In addition to demonstrating your ability to do the work, it's also important for you to be on the top of their minds. That circles us back to another reason why it's important to send cards, arrange happy hours, and have annual get-togethers.

But that's not enough. We need to come up with other, more specific ways to thank our referrals. I suggest you come up with a pipeline of standard, consistent ways to thank someone. That way, you don't have to scratch your head and waste precious billable time strategizing a unique thank you gift. I know lawyers who give out wine, some who mail gift cards, and others who have otherwise personalized "thank yous." Obviously, I tend to give out small-batch, hand-crafted decorated sugar cookies!

For that matter, don't limit your gift-giving to just referral instances. At the very least, get in the habit of sending out thank-you cards to committee members with whom you work on projects, judicial assistants who make your life easier, opposing counsel with whom you have worked. Yes, you read that right... opposing counsel. If you both fought hard for your respective clients and resolved the issues professionally, I encourage you to send a note to that lawyer, thanking him or her for their professionalism.

"But Babs, I don't have time to write all these notes you want me to!" You will if you make it super easy for yourself. I have on my desk an old-fashioned mail sorter, and in it, I have cards for many occasions: my firm note cards, birthday cards, thank you cards, and "Yay, You!" cards. I also always keep stamps handy. I have trained my team that I will put the name on a post-it (yeah, I have plenty) on the envelope, "John Q. Lawyer, Esq." and that's code for them to look up the address on floridabar.org. They then address the envelopes, ensure they are stamped (because I regularly forget to use them), and mail 'em out!

I also have a "traveling bag" of mail-stuff that resides in my car. That way, if I find myself killing time getting an oil change, my hair done, or a pedicure, I can take a few minutes and write some cards. In my bag are a smaller assortment of cards, lots of stamps, and two pens - one blue ink and one fun-colored ink for fun cards to write.

When I'm really on my A-game, I scroll through Facebook and take screenshots of life events my friends have posted for which I wish to send them cards. Then I move the photos to an album I've created called "cards to send" and I use that as a reminder. The trick to that, and why I say "when" I'm on top of things, is to send out those cards in a timely fashion. That can be tricky. I think in a perfect world, I would calendar fifteen minutes a day that I would dedicate to sending out cards, but I'm not that regimented.

9. LET ME KNOW!

Chances are pretty good I don't know you. At least not yet. To that end, please know that if I can ever help you with any of these ideas raised above, I'd be happy to! You can contact me at 407.672.1252 or barbara@bleachlaw.com. Part of being a successful law firm owner is knowing when to get help from others. I'm here for you if I can be of service. I started this chapter congratulating you on your decision to go out on your own, and I'll end it that same way. Being a business owner is incredibly rewarding. Being a law firm owner is another level of satisfying. I look forward to celebrating your many successes with you!

12 STEPS TO A PROFITABLE LAW PRACTICE

By Ernest Svenson

—

Ernest Svenson helps small firm lawyers transform their practices and improve their quality of life. His website (LawFirmAutopilot. com) shows them how to take advantage of technology to make more money, more easily so they can spend more time relaxing away from the office—even the so-called "dinosaur lawyers" who remain bewildered by email.

CHAPTER 3

12 Steps to a
Profitable Law Practice

By Ernest Svenson

Would you like a practice that's profitable and easy to manage? Well, I'm going to show you how to create one. My explanation will be most helpful for folks in small firms or with solo practices. But if you're about to start a new firm, it will be useful to you as well.

Lawyers have a hard time believing it's possible to have a practice that's both prosperous and easy to run. That's because most lawyers are completely frazzled. And some of the most frazzled ones are in small firms.

Why is this? Well, some pundits say the legal profession is now the victim of disruptive societal change. That sounds plausible at a superficial level. But the real reason is something less monumental, and something totally within our control.

Frankly, most of us aren't managing our practices very well. Not because of social upheaval. Not because we're inherently inept at running a business. But because we tend to focus most of our time and energy solving our clients' problems.

We ignore our business challenges, which is not good. Running a law firm presents tremendous business challenges, especially a small one with limited resources. A big key to running any business well is making effective use of your resources.

For example, time management is crucial. Time needs to be carefully managed, because it's the scarcest resource (and least replaceable) of all. Sadly, most of us don't manage our time as well as we should.

Another challenging resource is technology. And yes, technology can be confusing, especially with the dizzying array of options with which we're faced. But when managed properly, it can dramatically improve your practice.

So how do you manage technology properly? Well, that's what I'm going to show you. And once you learn the proper way, your law practice will be completely transformed. Imagine what your life will look like once that happens.

Imagine having so many great clients reaching out to you that you have to turn some away. Imagine spending about thirty minutes a week (at most) getting those potential clients to call you. Imagine making more money each year than you made the previous year, allowing you to steadily grow your practice in a way that's smooth and easy. Imagine having the luxury of spending much more time away from the office, relaxing and enjoying life.

That's what technology will do for you – once you learn how to use it properly.

Now maybe you're thinking, "But I can barely handle email, so how am I going to learn to leverage technology?" First, you don't need to master technology to leverage it. You only need to understand enough to hire the right people to help you. In other words, you don't have to push all the buttons yourself; you can hire people to push buttons for you (or automate the "button pushing," which is even better).

Listen, if you can follow a clear "process roadmap" – such as rules of civil procedure – then you are capable of radically improving your practice with common technology, most of which you already own. All you need is the right roadmap, which I'm going to give you. My process roadmap will work for you because it's already worked for hundreds of other lawyers just like you. It even worked for those who describe themselves as "dinosaur lawyers."

If you read on, I'll show you a well-defined twelve-step process for leveraging technology to transform your practice and improve your quality of life.

But, before we get into the process, let me briefly share the story of how I learned to leverage technology to create a thriving solo practice.

In 1987, after having spent two years clerking for a federal judge, I started working for a large New Orleans law firm. The firm had high-profile corporate clients in many different industries, and they charged their clients premium rates. So, not surprisingly, I was well-paid, even as a first-year associate.

Over the years, I worked on interesting cases and learned the art of practicing law. Mostly, the "art" involved managing voluminous information stored in voluminous boxes of paper. Paralegals did most of the grunt work, so it wasn't that taxing for me. Still, over the years I became less enthralled with the way I was practicing law.

Then the economy started hitting bumpy ground. Clients got nit-pickier about their bills, and recruiting new clients became more difficult. Meanwhile the firm's overhead kept climbing. So, everyone had to work harder for less money. The stress levels climbed, and I became dissatisfied. I started daydreaming about starting my own practice, preferably something simple, without the need for lots of staff to manage lots of paper.

One day a friend showed me how to scan paper into my computer, and I immediately saw how I could create a practice that was easy to manage, with low-overhead (i.e. less paper meant less required office space). But I still had the pesky problem of getting new clients.

The firm's institutional clients weren't going to hire a solo lawyer with no paralegals and a tiny office. Smaller businesses might, but how could I market to them and convince them to hire me? Well, the internet was the perfect medium, and I discovered its power mostly by accident.

In 2002, I started a weblog called "Ernie the Attorney." Although I did so as an experiment, it quickly got a lot of attention from all over the country (and even outside the U.S.). Then I started getting inquiries from potential clients who, having read my blog posts, decided they trusted me enough to hire me. However, they couldn't afford the high rates at my big firm. But – you got it – I knew how to solve that problem.

I gave up my big firm partnership, and simultaneously my big firm paycheck, to start my own solo practice. Of course, it wasn't easy at first, and I had many worried moments along the way, but it turned out to be a great decision. I used technology to do a lot of the work that I had previously delegated to paralegals and secretaries (who cost money, by the way). And I didn't have to work hardly at all to get new clients. My website brought me a steady stream of clients that loved working with me. I had more work than I could handle which made it easy not only to raise my rates, but also to be super picky about who I accepted as a client.

I could work as much as I wanted to, where I wanted to, and with whom I wanted to, mostly because of automation, outsourcing, and the internet. And while it was gratifying to have a practice that was profitable and easy to run, I found something even more fulfilling – showing other lawyers how to do the same thing. And for the last twelve years, that's what I've done.

Hopefully, you now understand why and how I can show you how to use technology to improve your practice. My advice is based on what I did in my practice, and what other lawyers have used in their practices. Because my recommendations are battle-tested, that is how you can have confidence they will work in your practice as well.

Okay, let's talk about the process. I mentioned there were twelve steps, and I'm going to go through each one so you can understand them. But first, let's talk about three phases that encompass those twelve steps. In general, these are phases that you need to go through as you transform your practice to make effective use of modern technology.

PHASE 1

First, you work on simplifying and lowering overhead. That means you'll start digitizing your bulky papers. This will enable you to use less office space, and not depend as much on human beings (i.e., paid staff) to shuffle paper. But you'll also save time and reduce stress because you'll be able to find critical information in seconds - anytime, anywhere. Best of all, eliminating paper sets you up for automating key workflows.

PHASE 2

This is where you get exponential increases in efficiency and cost savings. That's because you'll start harnessing the power of automation. Do you want to create documents with a few clicks and zero errors? How about getting great new clients in a predictable, steady stream even when you're busy, or asleep, or playing golf? Well, that's what automation can do for you, if you go about it in the right way.

PHASE 3

Finally, you'll learn to work virtually from anywhere with an internet connection. That will set you up to harness outsourcing. Not everything can be automated, but pretty much everything can be delegated. The talent pool of people to whom to delegate has never been bigger nor more easily accessible. Once you know the secrets of hiring virtual assistants, you can find smart, eager helpers with just a few keyboard tabs.

THE "12 STEPS"

Now let's drill down and discuss the twelve steps to transforming your practice by using technology.

1. MINDSET

First, you must develop the right mindset. Yes, we have to be realistic: technology can be a challenge for many lawyers. But the number one reason they struggle is because they don't approach technology in the right way. If you're intimidated or frustrated by technology, then the root of the problem is almost certainly how you're approaching it.

Most lawyers are haphazard in their approach. They might ask their tech-savvy lawyer friends for guidance, and they'll hire the first tech consultant they encounter. That's not an optimal approach. More likely, it's a path that inevitably leads to further frustration and failure.

The right mindset is one where you decide to make a strong commitment to leverage technology and then get the right kind of assistance.

2. A ROADMAP

You need a systematic approach for assessing the best technology options and then implementing them. You shouldn't just go from one shiny object to another. You need a basic roadmap that shows you how to leverage technology in a step-by-step way, which is what this chapter is showing you.

The next step is the most important one. Lawyers who don't follow this step are the ones who suffer the most in managing their practices.

3. SYSTEMS

You should have well-developed systems for running your law practice, and they should be documented. Of course, many lawyers do not have good systems. They have "loosey-goosey" systems. In other words, there's variation in how one staff member performs a task and how another person does it. I call this "chaotic variability," and it is an insidious problem.

Look, you need solid systems if you want to leverage technology in a way that makes your life easier, not harder. Documenting workflows is important with any kind of complex process, but it's crucial when using technology because chaotic variability is more dangerous when workflows are invisible (e.g., digital workflows). You cannot easily see disorganization inside a computer; it is essentially invisible – quietly and unobtrusively becoming a major disaster.

Creating systems is not hard. There are many books about this topic, but the one I most recommend is The *E-Myth* by Michael Gerber. It is a great overview of the various systems that all small businesses need to develop. Unfortunately, this book was not written for lawyers, but it will still give you 80% of the information you need.

For a law-focused book, I recommend John Fisher's *The Power of a System: How to Build the Injury Law Practice of Your Dreams*. Fisher is a New York personal injury attorney with a solo practice. He handles complex cases, and to be blunt, he makes a lot of money. But his practice is easier to manage because he uses systems and, more importantly, he documents them.

In fact, his book is his documentation. It is a detailed blueprint of the systems he uses in his day-to-day practice. He gives it to every new staff person who comes to work for him so that they know precisely what they need to do without him having to repeatedly coach them. If you want to know what your documented systems should look like, read Fisher's book (it's available on Amazon in Kindle format, or from him directly if you want the hardbound version - http://ultimateinjurylaw.com).

4. TECH ASSISTANCE

As you work on taking full advantage of technology, you are wise to obtain expert assistance. You will need help selecting the best options and then prioritizing them. Besides not having systems in place, this is probably the biggest error that leads to failure for small firm lawyers. It is imperative that you find the best people to help you manage technology.

Your "tech-savvy" friend is not a good choice, because you need professional guidance, not amateurish help. The best professional is one who not only knows a lot about technology, but also has specific experience advising lawyers in various practice areas.

I know many smart lawyers who are adept at using technology to help them run their firm, but are not as adept at helping other lawyers. Why? Because their perspective is too narrow; they only understand what worked for them. They have a hammer and, to them, every tech problem looks like the nails they pounded into their own practice. Avoid those people.

You need trustworthy technology consultants to help you make good choices and to help you implement those choices. Now let's talk about some of the key technology choices you should make.

5. PAPERLESS LAWYERING

If you want to streamline your practice and reduce clutter and chaos, you need to stop managing information and in paper form. Digital information is cheaper to store, easier to transmit, and can be automated more easily. Digitizing paper is about more than just scanning, because when you shift to a paperless practice, you'll need to make sure you have solid systems for managing that digital information.

Now, you probably already have some systems in place for your word processing files and maybe mail. But you need to get more strategic and more systematic when you shed paper. This does not mean that you'll never deal with paper again - rather, just that you're dealing with a lot less of it. Furthermore, your main information managing system will be digitally based as opposed to paper-based.

To learn more about creating a paperless practice you can go to the paperlesschase.com and sign up for the free, one-page guide to going paperless. If you do, I'll follow up with a free 10-part email course that will walk you through everything. It will explain what scanner to get, how to organize digital documents, what documents you need to keep in paper form, etc.

6. PDF SKILLS

One of those common questions lawyers often have is: what format should I scan my documents to? The answer is the PDF format. From now on, just think of PDFs as digital paper. As you probably know, e-filing is now mandatory in every federal court, and it's increasingly being adopted in state courts as well. Original documents filed in the record are no longer paper documents – they are PDF files. So, PDF is the format to use when digitizing and organizing your documents.

There is a lot to learn about PDFs, and the more you learn, the smoother you'll make the transition to a paperless practice. Plus, you'll feel more comfortable eliminating the paper version of the document once you know how to effectively work with PDFs.

7. THE CLOUD

As you release yourself from excessive dependency on paper, you will want the freedom to access your information anytime, anywhere - even when you're out of the office. And that means you need to embrace the cloud.

The cloud is mysterious to many lawyers as well as laypersons, but actually, it is a pretty simple concept. Basically, it means you can use the internet to make transferring digital files fast, simple, and easy. When you send someone an email with an attachment, you are using the cloud. But, what most of us mean when we say "embrace the cloud" is you should start storing some of your information in the cloud, so you don't have to ask someone in the office to email you a file.

You can use cloud services like Dropbox or Google Drive to host some or all of your digital files on their servers; then you can access those files anytime you want from anywhere, even if you only have your smartphone or an iPad. So, think of the cloud as universal access to all of your documents and files. If that information is still only in paper form, then it is not going to be available via the cloud, and that's why I said you need to convert all of your documents to PDF and upload them to Dropbox, Box.com, your practice management software, or anywhere else online. I'm sure others will recommend this scanner as well, but I highly recommend the Fujitsu ScanSnap iX500, as it will scan directly into your Dropbox folder, making the process more streamlined.

8. AUTOMATION

As I mentioned earlier, the real power of modern digital technology comes from automation. We know that digital automation can be used to turn on lights at a certain time or send us reminders, but it can also be used for many other things that we previously could not even imagine. For example, digital automation can be used to attract clients via the web. Then, add them to your email campaigns and offer high quality content that helps answer their pain points. Once they see you're providing value and knowledge, it should help add authority and trust.

To setup a sophisticated automation workflow, I would recommend using InfusionSoft. However, I would also recommend finding an expert that specializes in InfusionSoft, as it is not the easiest to set up the first time. Of course, this is sophisticated automation and not entry-level stuff. Focus first on automation that involves common office work, and that will help you develop an understanding of how to automate more complex tasks.

The most common office tasks for lawyers involve generating documents: pleadings, contracts, affidavits, email correspondences, and routine forms.

Much of those text-generating workflows can be automated. The key is determining which of those workflows should be automated and, among those, which should be automated first.

9. SECURITY

The more we rely on digital automation and information, the more we need to pay attention to how to keep it secure. Part of security is making sure that the data is not inadvertently deleted or somehow lost. Another part is protecting our data against interception by bad guys, also known as hackers. Certain practice areas are more prone to attacks by hackers, but the most common attacks affect every kind of law firm.

Unfortunately, there are a lot of misconceptions and misinformation related to security, some perpetuated by consultants who make money off selling security services. They find it easier to sell their services when people are confused or scared.

Here is the main thing to be aware of – hackers are dangerous for two reasons: 1) they have automated their most common attacks, and 2) they use very effective psychological manipulation to gain entry into your computer, which they have automated as well.

Once you understand how they use psychology, you will be able to prevent 80% of the most common attacks, even when the hackers come up with new variations.

10. MOBILE LAWYERING

"Mobile lawyering" simply means practicing law without constantly being tethered to a desk in your office. Embracing the cloud, which we mentioned earlier, is what makes this possible. Today, you no longer need to remain tethered to your office, unless that is the best place to get your work done.

Sometimes we have to work away from the office because it is inconvenient to drive into the office. Sometimes we find ourselves stuck in a client's office or in another lawyer's conference room. Instead of twiddling our thumbs, we can open up laptop or get out our smartphone and bang out emails that need to be answered.

If you are in court, you may need to quickly pull up a case your opponent cited, or find case law that contradicts their assertion. When you have "always anywhere" access to your information, then you can do that. The amount of work you can do with just a smartphone or a laptop and an internet connection is amazing.

11. OUTSOURCING

Ideally, you should only be doing the things that require a law license to do. Everything else should be automated or delegated, and a lot of what you should delegate can be outsourced to people who either work part-time or full-time. Hiring assistants who can work virtually using cloud tools is the way to go. If you have solid systems that you've documented, then handing work off to virtual assistants is a piece of cake. Chris Ducker's book, *Virtual Freedom*, will give you the full scoop on how to use virtual assistants to grow your practice smoothly and steadily. It is not focused on law, but I highly recommend it.

12. ONLINE MARKETING

You must learn to market your practice online. This is the thing that will have the greatest long-term payoff. If you do this right, your practice could be two or three times more profitable, but without any increase in workload. The internet is where all the gold is, and you need to learn to mine it. I won't go into too much detail here, as I know future chapters are covering this in great length. But what I can tell you is this: follow their advice, and you should hopefully get new clients visiting your website daily, and - most importantly – hiring you.

Increasingly, people are looking to the internet when they need to hire a lawyer. Today, most people looking for a lawyer use the internet as part of their search process or as part of their evaluation process. Therefore, having a website is crucial for lawyers now.

How do you attract potential clients who are using the internet to search for legal services? First learn how to market online, which doesn't mean having a fancy, expensive website (which unfortunately is what most lawyers believe).

So, what should you do to learn proper online marketing? First, learn the principles of marketing, and then apply the ones that work best for small businesses to the Internet.

The best kind of marketing for small businesses is something called direct-response marketing. This method is incredibly effective in any medium (e.g. direct mail, billboard advertising, TV, etc.), not just the internet. Direct-response marketing is appealing for lawyers who feel awkward promoting themselves. In other words, if you're an introvert who doesn't like to go to networking events (like me), you'll love direct-response marketing. In short, direct-response marketing means you are asking for a reply. If you advertise in a magazine, you may ask the reader to take an action and call a special number. If you send a letter in the mail, you may ask them to visit a certain page on your site. If you send an email, you may end with asking them to reply back to schedule a consultation. Either way, you want to track your marketing efforts so you can track the ROI (return on investment) per campaign. Always include a call to action, and always ask for a response or reply. When you add in urgency and scarcity, you will be surprised what it could do. For example, increased revenue by sending an email out that you are running a 24-hour holiday promotion where your fees are cut in half for new clients. Or running a 48-hour promotion where you give free one-hour consultations to anyone – new or existing clients. The options are endless; it all comes down to your creativity and execution.

The best and fastest way to learn more about direct-response marketing is from Dan Kennedy's book, *No B.S. Direct Marketing*. This book will show you how it works, and even how it works for lawyers.

CONCLUSION
So, that's the process in a nutshell. Get help from the right people and work through those steps in an orderly fashion. Don't get impatient. And, above all, avoid the haphazard approach that many lawyers use. That's how you will create an incredibly satisfying practice – one that's highly profitable and also easy to manage.

UNDERSTANDING THE NEW LEGAL CONSUMER AND THRIVING IN THE REVIEW ECONOMY

By Dan Lear

—

Dan Lear is a lawyer, blogger, and legal industry gadfly. As a technology-focused business lawyer, Dan has advised companies from startups to the Fortune 100, helping to develop agreements and terms for early cloud services offerings well before "the cloud" was an everyday norm.

CHAPTER 4
Understanding the New Legal Consumer and Thriving in the Review Economy

By Dan Lear

Most lawyers say that word-of-mouth referrals are a central part of their marketing strategy. However, data from the online marketing firm Brightlocal suggests that more people leave online reviews than give reviews or referrals in person (65% vs. 34%). Additionally, far more people trust online reviews, specifically 80%, than those who do not. In order to thrive in the 21st-century economy, lawyers need to understand the modern legal consumer as well as how to communicate effectively with them.

Avvo's consumer research paints a fascinating picture of the new legal consumer.

First, the new legal consumer is informed. Today's legal consumer has access to more legal information than any legal consumer ever. And they're taking full advantage of that information. Forty-two percent of new legal consumers are at least initially researching their legal issue online. Most importantly, 31% are researching lawyers. One in five legal consumers believes that, with enough research, they can know what a lawyer knows.

This may strike fear in the heart of lawyers, or cause them to roll their eyes at the notion of "internet-informed" consumers, but lawyers' reactions to this behavior are largely irrelevant. The fact of the matter is that this information is and will continue to be available to consumers. They are making and will continue to make use of it. As a result, lawyers need to understand these consumers so they can know what kinds of services to offer them and how to go about it.

Today's legal consumers are also connected. They're privy not only to their friends' opinions and recommendations regarding legal services or lawyers, but also to strangers' opinions and experiences, and details and thoughts on specific lawyers, judges, the legal system, and/or the law itself.

Today's legal consumer is taking full advantage of the wide variety of options that the internet provides. Whether they are using Avvo's question and answer forum to get an answer to simple legal questions, the low-cost 15-minute advice sessions, or the dozens of other similar types of services on the web, consumers have access to a wide variety of free and low-cost limited legal information and advice.

If consumers want more than just advice or information, they can also find unbundled and fixed-fee services frequently available online - and often without the need to ever physically meet with a lawyer. Research shows that consumers find these options appealing: 47% respond positively to hiring an attorney only to review an already prepared document, and 76% find the idea of a fixed-fee service appealing.

Finally, just as technology has radically changed the way that all of us do just about everything, it's changing the way the new legal consumer tackles legal issues and finds a lawyer. For example, the new legal consumer doesn't always come to a lawyer first when they think they have a legal issue. Just as the "path-to-purchase" for consumers in every sector is now highly unpredictable, the "path-to-purchase" for legal consumers is similarly convoluted.

Consumers may bounce from personal recommendations to free advice sessions, to online questions and answers, to product reviews, to lawyer reviews, to phoning a lawyer and back again all before deciding to ultimately engage a lawyer. The good news for lawyers, according to our research, is that consumers do this with relative regularity. Over 40% of all legal consumers hire a lawyer at some point during the course of the journey of resolving their legal issue.

So what can a lawyer do with this information? What can law firms do today to make the most of the opportunities afforded by the attitudes of the new legal consumer? One thing is understanding and capitalizing on online reviews. Research shows that the new legal consumer cares more about consumer reviews than where a lawyer went to law school or the judge the lawyer clerked for. As a result, lawyers who want to engage the new legal consumer must understand and effectively utilize the consumer review economy.

The first step in capitalizing on the consumer review economy is for lawyers to actively cultivate a culture of feedback with their clients. With a sea of good reviews, one bad one fades into the background instead of looking like an eyesore.

There are lots of ways that lawyers can encourage their clients to leave them good reviews. One way is for lawyers to ask their friends for reviews. Many lawyers have clients with whom they have developed a close personal relationship, perhaps over a number of years. Those clients are excellent resources in starting to develop a proactive online reputation strategy.

Another simple tip is reminding clients in a number of places to leave a review. For example, a lawyer could leave a simple message in their email footer saying something like: "Satisfied with your service? Leave us a review on Avvo." and a link back to the lawyer's Avvo profile. Another way is a simple follow-up email at the conclusion of a matter with a request for a client to leave a review.

Finally, when all else fails, use alcohol. OK, that's a joke, but only sort of. There's a lawyer in Chicago who holds a holiday party for all of her clients at the end of the year. As clients arrive at the party, she asks clients to record a video testimonial for her use on her website. With just a handful of those video reviews, this lawyer has already taken care of a good chunk of her annual online reputation management activities.

Many lawyers are hesitant to embrace online reviews. Beyond the fact that feedback can be scary and hard for anyone, Larry Richard, a researcher on lawyer personality, has shown that 90% of all lawyers score in the bottom half of the population for the personality trait of "resilience." Loosely defined, resilience is the ability to pick oneself up after falling down or being knocked down.

For anyone, getting less-than-positive feedback about their work can hurt – and doubly so for lawyers who struggle with resilience. Lawyers need to remember that feedback can be very valuable. Feedback is a consumers' way of telling a lawyer how they can improve their business. Lawyers will be much more likely to embrace a culture of feedback if they understand the value of it.

The final key to cultivating a culture of feedback for your firm is to embrace feedback internally as well. This is a bit of an aside, but open and transparent information is the foundation of the modern workplace. Employees need to feel that they can speak up and share their opinion and feedback without being punished. By understanding the value of feedback and embracing it, lawyers can build and make the most of a culture of feedback both externally and internally.

Lawyers who wish to thrive in the new economy must understand and capitalize on the opportunities offered by the online legal consumer. By understanding who this consumer is and by embracing the way that the new legal consumer finds and uses information – online reviews being a prime example – lawyers will grow their practices today and into the future.

HOW TO START OR TRANSITION INTO AN ECO FRIENDLY PRACTICE

By Aastha Madaan

Aastha Madaan is the owner and founder of Madaan Law, P.C., where she focuses her practice on business law and estate planning. Aastha often writes and speaks on the topics of cultural competency in the practice of law. She is an advocate for access to legal services and volunteers her time on boards to create better access through legal insurance and innovation.

CHAPTER 5

How to Start or Transition into An Eco Friendly Practice

By Aastha Madaan

Although I have always thought of myself as an environmentally conscious person, I did not truly understand what that meant until 2014. That year, thanks to social media, I discovered the zero-waste lifestyle. This chapter will cover the basics of having an environmentally conscious practice, including: (1) what it means to "go green;" (2) what challenges there are in workplace eco-consciousness; and (3) the steps you can take to make changes in every part of your practice.

WHAT IT MEANS TO "GO GREEN"

"Going Green" is more than a catchphrase. We live in a "use and throw away" world. Knowing the impact this lifestyle has on our future should be enough to propel us to change. According to some reports, every year, the United States generates approximately 230 million tons of trash. In fact, an individual creates 4.6 pounds of trash per day, but less than one-quarter of this trash is recycled. Therefore, the remaining three-quarters of this trash is incinerated or sent off to landfills. Each day more than 60 million plastic water bottles are thrown away, most of which end up in a landfill. Even the ones that do not end up in landfills require a lot of energy, water, and other resources to re-create them into another product.

If each person were to cut their daily waste in half, imagine the impact! The change begins with changing your mindset so you are conscious of things you are doing that can impact the environment. I hope that you no longer mindlessly throw away an empty plastic bottle, or that you perhaps eat one less bag of candy at the office, because that waste will end up in landfills.

The change begins with sending fewer items to landfills, wasting and using fewer resources, and simply practicing environmental mindfulness.

CHALLENGES

There are several challenges to making the change, but the biggest challenge is your own mindset. We do not think of our workplace as a place of permanence. We think of it as a temporary stop, even though we spend more than one-third of the hours in a day there. For our home, we purchase steel utensils, pans, plates, cloth towels, and fancy jugs that infuse strawberries and cucumbers into our drinking water. But for our law practice, we buy Styrofoam cups and plastic forks because our office is not a place into which we put TLC. Once you start thinking of your office as a place of permanence, as a place that has an impact on your life and on the environment, you will start investing more effectively and becoming more responsible and mindful of the things you do at your office.

WHERE TO BEGIN?

Once you have recognized the need for a change in mindset, where do you begin? Where you begin will depend on whether you are starting a new practice, or transitioning your current practice into an environmentally friendly one.

If you are beginning a new practice or moving to a new office space, you have a great opportunity to create processes and habits early on to adopt a new work-lifestyle.

If you already have an established practice, rethink your relationship with your clients or potential clients. Assess each contact you have with the client, as well as any in-between prep time and resources you use. This means assessing whether you are still taking notes during the consultation on a yellow pad. Maybe it's time to switch to a conventional device like an iPad Pro or Microsoft Surface Pro. Below is a comprehensive list of categories to keep in mind as you reform the way you practice law.

Shopping for your New Office: Once you have your office space and are seeking to decorate it, consider purchasing gently used furniture and filing cabinets from a website like Craigslist, Facebook Marketplace, freecycle.org, or a liquidation sale. This can save you money as well as give a second chance at life to all those resources so they don't end up in landfills.

Start from the Beginning: Is your office still taking phone messages on paper? Consider switching to an online messenger system. A no-cost and easy switch is to create a Google Form (Google.com/forms) with just a few fields for your phone answering person to use. That way you get a notification every time someone leaves a message for you. You can also consider having an email template you can easily fill out to save time. Or, if you use a case management software like PracticePanther, you should DEFINITELY add all your notes from every call under the Contact or Matter profiles so everyone in the firm can see what you spoke to them about. It's impossible to remember everything you said to everyone, so having a good system in place will help you and your team as you grow.

Note-Taking: Yes, I realize that yellow pads are a hallmark of a law practice. I love to take notes by hand too, but I have now developed a habit of taking notes in PracticePanther. I create a Matter for each person I speak with and take notes for the initial meeting within that Matter. They are easy to retrieve and saved in one convenient place, so I am not digging through a filing cabinet, file, or stack of papers on my desk. One thing that helped with this was to switch from a desktop while taking notes to having an iPad or Microsoft Surface Pro to take notes.

Retainer Agreements: Once the consultation is completed, you may sign that client up (which includes a retainer agreement) on paper and have them send you a check for a retainer/trust account payment. An easy alternative is to switch to Adobe Pro DC, which lets you send an unlimited number of documents for a low monthly fee. You can use PracticePanther to send invoices and accept online payments via PantherPayments, powered by LawPay, which is what I prefer to use.

Correspondence with Clients: I used to work at a firm that would send the client an email and then a hard copy of each letter/correspondence. The opposing counsel did the same, and before we knew it, we were racking up boxes of files and papers for each matter. The easy solution is to send some correspondence (such as pleadings) electronically by using online client portals.

If you have a practice management software with a client portal, you know how easy it is to send invoices, documents, and secure messages to your clients.

Internal Documents: Paper is an interesting vice. It is relatively easy to recycle, yet the majority of us simply throw it in the trash. I see people taking notes on printing paper and then discarding the paper in the trash. Paper accounts for 35% of commercial waste and it's important to remember that any recycling also uses energy, resources, and manpower. So, to the extent that we can avoid using recyclable items in the first place, we should.

Easy ways to transition to using less, or even no, paper are:

1. Transition to cloud storage.
2. Instead of printing emails, save them as PDF's, which you can do directly from most email services. Simply find the "print" button and choose "PDF" as the preferred method of delivery.
3. Get into the habit of making an "EMAILS" folder in each client folder, further subdivided as needed, for example: "Emails from/to Client," "Emails from/to Opposing Counsel," "Emails from/to adjustor," etc.
4. Set your printers to automatically print two-sided.
5. Stop buying yellow pads and start taking notes on a tablet or some other electronic device.

Mail-Sending: Some easy changes for sending mail in a more environmentally-friendly way are printing directly on an envelope instead of printing labels, and paying a printer to print envelopes with your firm's logo so you don't waste labels. And of course, try to only mail items you cannot email.

Mail-Receiving: When you register as a business, often your business address and other information is gathered and sold for marketing purposes. This means you will receive junk mail and advertisements within days of starting your business. Over 100 million trees end up as junk mail every year in the United States. To avoid contributing to this problem, you can register your personal and professional addresses on a website called www.dmachoice. org to remove yourself from receiving mailers and other junk mail. It takes some time to go into effect, but it has a huge impact. Another thing you can do is when you take a new case, you and opposing counsel can stipulate to receive mail and other correspondence via email.

Office Recycling: Even if you have executive suites, you can easily recycle. Most office buildings recycle their paper waste, so simply ask them to provide a small bin for recycling paper. And think beyond paper when you are thinking of recycling. Have an e-recycling bin or box in the break room. Your office will have batteries, cords, USB keys, and other electronics that will stop working. Give yourself and the people in your office an alternative to just tossing them in the trash. Almost all cities and counties have free e-recycling programs and drop-off points. You can easily Google these or call your city to ask when and where you can drop off e-recycling.

Green Vendors: If you are using vendors like a process server, printers etc., ask them about their policies. In California, courts use "e-filing" and only certain vendors are approved to do it. When I e-file using my vendor, I request that they send me electronic copies only and not mail me extra paper copies. I purchase recycled paper and recycled ink when I order new business cards. After I am done using the cards, my printer will take back the box they came in and reuse it.

Change Up Break Time: You can save money and reduce your carbon footprint by eliminating plastic utensils and cups from your office. In lieu of paper or plastic cups, purchase glass cups and keep stainless steel utensils in the kitchen. You can wash and reuse these cups and utensils instead of dumping a plastic cup in the trash after one use. Create good habits for yourself and the people working with you.

Networking: The biggest way to make networking environmentally friendly is to use the resources you already have! If you have a smartphone, have your LinkedIn app and your QR reader ready to go. Connect with people immediately and skip taking the business card. Better yet, take a photo of the card. There are also apps that will scan a business card and save the contact information for you. ABBYY Business Card Reader (Apple and Android), CamCard, and PrestoBizCard are just some of the apps available now to make it easier to save contact information from business cards.

Tap into social media as an immediate way to connect. When someone tells you he/she practices law, ask if they have a Twitter or other social media page. Connecting with people through social media is one of the best ways to maintain relationships and interact with people.

Keeping Records: Leverage technology for keeping track of receipts and recycle them. Create a folder on your phone and take photos of receipts or create a doc and save it. At the end of the year, all your expenses will be saved in one folder! In PracticePanther, you can scan all your receipts to a particular client matter.

These are just some of the ways to incorporate waste-free habits into your work life and law practice. The key is to constantly learn. Most things that create waste will have a waste-free alternative. Good luck going green!

—

SOCIAL MEDIA, MARKETING & SEO

TOP 10 MOST COST-EFFECTIVE MARKETING TIPS FOR LAWYERS

By David Bitton

—

As an author, CLE speaker, and founder of PracticePanther.com, David is dedicated to automating law firms with the help of today's technology. He's revolutionizing the legal industry by helping lawyers get more done in less time using PracticePanther's practice management software.

CHAPTER 6

Top 10 Most Cost-Effective Marketing Tips for Lawyers

By David Bitton

Marketing is an integral part of operating a successful law firm. You must have a successful marketing strategy if you expect to compete with other attorneys in your target area. "Selling yourself" does not come naturally for all lawyers. However, marketing does not require that you have an outgoing personality or a lot of money. It does require that you put some thought into how you can market yourself and your law firm in a way that will attract new clients as well as keep current clients returning when they need legal services. The key to a successful marketing strategy is to focus on the things that you do well.

For example, if you are an excellent chef and you are a real estate attorney, consider hosting regular dinner parties for local realtors and mortgage lenders. This will allow you to showcase your abilities in the kitchen while gently reminding them of your strong abilities as a real estate attorney. On the other hand, if you do not know anything about a kitchen other than how to organize leftover takeout in the fridge, but you are an amateur wine connoisseur, consider hosting regular wine tastings at your law firm. Using your strengths to market yourself and your law firm is the most effective means of building your reputation and generating new business.

THE TOP 10 LIST:

We have searched high and low to find the best marketing tips for lawyers. Our list does not in any way include every marketing tool available to attorneys and law firms. However, our list offers some creative ways you can market your law firm using your strengths without breaking your advertising budget.

1. Write blogs that appeal to the average person

If you do not have a blog, begin one immediately. Try and refrain from writing blog posts aimed at other attorneys, unless that's your target market. Your blog should provide useful information to your target audience. For example, if you are a bankruptcy attorney, writing about bankruptcy exemptions will not attract as much attention as telling someone how they can protect their property from creditors. Write your blog as if you were telling a close family member how you can help them rather than trying to write a legal commercial aimed at someone with an advanced degree.

2. Skip holiday greeting cards

Many attorneys use the holidays to connect with their clients and potential clients. However, your card will simply be one of many. Instead, pick another occasion to reach out. For example, if your law firm is in Plant City, Florida, you may want to send a greeting card with a strawberry recipe to coincide with the annual Strawberry Festival. If you practice in Keystone, South Dakota, send a greeting card celebrating President's Day. The key is to pick a local event or holiday to celebrate so people will associate you with your location. Or, do as Barbara Leach said, and choose a random day like Valentine's Day to send your cards out.

3. Collect business cards

Handing your business card to potential contacts at meetings or other functions usually results in your cards being thrown in the trash or tossed in a desk drawer and forgotten. Instead, collect business cards from other attendees and send your information to each person by email or "snail" mail within a few days. Even better, add them to your email marketing software like MailChimp so you can send them automated campaigns every few weeks to stay top of mind.

4. Use social media

We won't touch too much on social media, as there are plenty of experts in this book that go into much greater detail. It is important to at least note that if you do not have a social media presence, you need one. If you are uncomfortable using social media, hire a professional SEO company to "tweet" and "post" for you. Social media cannot be ignored for most practice areas. If you don't have the time, use a software like Hootsuite to schedule multiple posts for the future so you can set it and forget it. This way, your clients or potential clients can see that your law firm is alive and active online. The worst thing you can do is have six fans on your Facebook page and have three posts from three years ago.

5. Extend professional courtesy

To reiterate what Barbara Leach mentioned earlier, other attorneys who practice in different areas of law can become your best referral sources. If another attorney or his/her family member needs professional assistance, consider taking the case for free, or at least at a heavy discount. This is an easy way to gain referrals in the future, as the business will come right back around one day.

6. Offer your services as a speaker

Speaking engagements are the same as free advertising, provided you offer valuable information in an entertaining fashion. If you are comfortable with public speaking, seek out speaking engagements to market yourself and your law firm. When people see you speaking, you are automatically a trustworthy source of knowledge, and they will most likely see you as the best option to help them with a current or future case.

7. Join professional groups and organizations

Regardless of how long you have been in practice, networking is still an important marketing tool for lawyers. Steve Fretzin will cover this later in much greater detail as the business development expert, but we simply recommend joining local, state, and national organizations and groups related your specific area of law.

8. Teach a CLE class

If you work with other attorneys, get your class approved by your state bar for CLE credit. It's actually not as hard as you think to get your course approved for CLE credits. Call your state bar or search their website for a CLE accreditation form. It's normally just a one-page form, and you should hear back within two to four weeks, if not sooner. We've offered classes with and without CLE credits, but there was always a significant increase in attendance when credits were offered…and especially when food was offered too!

9. Volunteer

Volunteering in your community is an excellent way to give back, help others, and market your law firm. Volunteering opens the doors to countless opportunities, and it can also be a fun company activity. Ask everyone in your firm to meet you on a weekend, and turn it into a team-bonding activity. Who knows, you might even meet a new client while you are serving food, cleaning up a park, helping seniors, or delivering meals.

10. Use the local news and media outlets

Pay attention to news stories in your community. If you have genuine expertise in an area related to local news, offer to answer questions or provide information on the subject matter. Let reporters and others know you are willing to be a "source" for more information related to trending news stories. Mitch Jackson briefly discusses this later in the book, but he uses the term "news-jacking." This is the process of writing a blog post, or social media post, or recording a Facebook Live video about your legal thoughts on a popular news story. Mitch even got picked up by local news outlets and has been featured on multiple news stations as a result! Now, he's the go-to legal expert for many local news stations any time similar stories appear. Imagine the free publicity!

Things to Avoid When Marketing Yourself and Your Law Firm

- Bragging about yourself – This is a definite "turn off" for almost everyone.
- When asked what you do for a living, don't say "I am an attorney." Instead, tell the person what you do. For example, when talking to a mortgage lender, instead of saying "I am a real estate attorney," say "I handle foreclosure actions." Or when talking to a realtor or someone looking to buy or sell a house, say, "I help people purchase and sell homes."
- Don't network only with other attorneys. Broaden your network to include anyone related to your area of law.

- Don't post random, useless social media or blogs posts. You must offer value and high-quality content. Everything you place online must speak directly to potential clients and provide information that makes them want to get more knowledge on the subject.
- Don't tackle marketing if you are not comfortable with the concept. If you have no idea how to market yourself, hire a professional.

You Can Do It!

Every attorney can do something to market themselves and their law firm. Take as many steps as you can to market your law firm to attract more people. Use your strengths and/or hire a professional to get your name out there to bring in new business. Follow up on all contacts you meet and use your calendar or any software to set reminders. All the time spent marketing should hopefully equate to many new clients who will be worth all the hard work, time, and effort.

CHAPTER 7

MARKETING YOUR LAW PRACTICE - START WITH YOUR CLIENTS

By Allison C. Shields

Allison C. Shields is the President of Legal Ease Consulting, Inc., which offers coaching, consulting and copywriting services for lawyers and law firms. She focuses in the areas of marketing, social media, business development, productivity, practice management, and client service.

CHAPTER 7

Marketing Your Law Practice - Start with Your Clients

By Allison C. Shields

If you want to focus on only one thing to improve your marketing, focus on your audience – who you are marketing to. Sound simple? Perhaps, but look at a lot of lawyer marketing materials and it becomes clear that many ignore this basic principle.

START WITH YOUR CLIENTS

First, get excruciatingly clear on who your best clients are and why. Create an ideal client profile so that you can easily recognize potential clients who may fit into this category, and so that you can describe your ideal clients succinctly and consistently. This will help you educate your referral sources and help them to spot your ideal clients so that they immediately know who to refer to you.

A lot of lawyers make the mistake of trying to target too broad an audience for fear of turning business away. But instead of attracting more clients, a poorly identified ideal client results in a watered-down message that loses its impact and fails to elicit a response.

When you have a good picture of who your ideal clients are, you can move forward to determine what is important to them, where to find them, how to attract them, how best to serve them, what processes and procedures you should put in place to serve them, which employees will work best with those clients, and more.

WHO ARE YOUR BEST CLIENTS?

The value of a client isn't measured solely by the size of the case or the size of your fee. Valuable clients can be those who have realistic expectations, respect your advice, and/or or want the best service. Perhaps your ideal client is one who works with you on a case – or perhaps it's just the opposite and you prefer clients who leave you alone and let you do what you do best. Maybe your best clients are simply those who will be 'raving fans' and generate lots of referrals for your practice.

Review your past and present client lists and ask yourself these questions:

- Which clients did you work best with?
- Which were the most lucrative for the firm?
- Which were the best sources of additional business or referrals?
- Which clients were the most difficult?
- Which ones failed to pay or did not take your advice?
- Which ones brought you matters that didn't fit into your strengths?

Make a list of the characteristics of good and bad clients. Once you have a preliminary idea of what a 'high value' client means to you, they will be easier to spot. This takes some in-depth work, but it is well worth it. When you become skilled at defining and identifying high-value clients, you waste less time and energy on lower value clients that sap your energy; cause you undue stress; and cost you money, time or other resources.

TALK ABOUT YOUR CLIENTS, NOT YOURSELF

Listen to how most lawyers talk about their practices (or read their websites, social media posts, and other marketing materials): it's all about them, and very little about the people they serve. This is a mistake. Clients care more about themselves and their problems than about you. Why not change the focus of your marketing to be more aligned with the clients' interests?

Your marketing message should create an association for the people you are speaking to so that they either identify themselves as your ideal clients or immediately think of someone else who needs your services.

Instead of focusing your marketing message on you, focus on who you serve and what they struggle with (or what opportunities they seek to capitalize on).

BUILD A BUYER PROFILE

Use your marketing message to speak directly to your ideal clients, rather than to a general audience. Think about who is your ideal customer. What do they look like? What problems do they need help with? What is the name you will associate with them? Let's assume your ideal client in your head is named Bob. Bob is in the process of getting divorced, he has 2 kids, no prenuptial agreement, and needs your help badly. He is your typical buyer profile.

Instead of making a general statement ("Family lawyer for everyone!") to get someone's attention, identifying them by their buyer persona ("Males aged 25-45 that are in the process of getting divorced and have children") is much more effective. Your ideal client will be tuned in to that information because it's very specific to them. Your marketing should do the same for your clients. Make them think you're talking directly to them. This will also have the effect of weeding out everyone who is not Bob, and to whom your message does not apply.

You need to be intimately familiar with who your clients are. The better you know the clients you're seeking to attract, the better your marketing efforts will be. Creating a client profile is a good way to develop that knowledge.

Keep in mind that whether your practice focuses on individuals or businesses, all of your clients are people. If you have a business to business practice, the decision-makers are still human beings you need to connect with in order to get their work.

When creating your ideal client profile, remember that you may have a different "ideal client" for different areas of practice or services you provide. Some areas to explore include the four P's: **Psychographics, Patterns** for choosing legal services, client **Problems**, and your **Positioning**.

PSYCHOGRAPHICS

Psychographics are the attitudes, aspirations, values, goals, and other psychological characteristics of your ideal clients. Tuning in to your ideal clients' psychographics is a powerful way to connect with clients, but lawyers rarely take the time to do so.

You may find that your clients are very different demographically, yet have similar psychographic profiles. Psychographics, while less tangible than demographics, are much more accurate in predicting which people or businesses will relate best to your particular message, method, or solution.

Psychographics include things like: your client's mission, goals, philosophy or values; their reputation in the industry or community; their management or communication style; integrity; or litigation history. They include any belief or value that your clients strongly identify with; they do not necessarily have to relate directly to the client's business or legal matter.

PATTERNS

An important part of profiling your ideal client is determining when and how they choose legal services. Knowing that your clients are more likely to make the decision to hire a lawyer at certain times of the year, as the result of specific triggering events, or upon receipt of specific types of information, can help you plan your services and your marketing strategy. Learn why your clients hire you, what kinds of service providers they prefer, and what similar services they have used to better target your marketing message.

PROBLEMS

Another effective way to connect with clients is to identify the problems they face. Everyone wants their problems to be solved. If you can identify what the client perceives their problem to be (as opposed to what you - or other lawyers - think their problem is), you'll get the potential client's attention quickly and start gaining their trust. Identify the problems themselves, as well as the symptoms of the problems that your clients commonly experience, and how clients typically describe them. Use that information in your marketing.

Questions to ask include:

- What do your clients want or need?
- How do clients talk about their problems, wants, and needs?
- Are your clients seeking to achieve a specific result?
- What are the underlying emotions your clients typically experience when facing the kinds of legal problems you solve?

Use the language your clients use when crafting your marketing messages, writing copy for your website, posting on social media, or discussing at a cocktail party what you do. Put yourself in your clients' shoes. If you can do that, your marketing will instantly stand out and help you build relationships.

POSITIONING

Once you've ascertained the beliefs, values, and goals (psychographics), analyzed the problems, and determined when and how your ideal clients choose legal services, you need to position yourself properly to get your message in front of the right people. The "right people" may be the clients themselves, the clients' trusted advisors, or other referral sources. Your client profile should help you to position yourself in front of the right people if it includes an analysis of the places your ideal clients and referral sources gather.

To find out where the right people are, ask questions like:

- What do your ideal clients read?
- What do they watch or listen to?
- Who influences them?
- What kinds of advisors do they seek?
- Which websites do they visit?
- Where and how do they participate in social media?
- Where and how do your ideal clients seek out information?
- What professional associations do they belong to?
- What types of events do they attend?
- What causes do they care about?

If you don't already know the answers to these questions, ask your best clients, or do some research on your existing clients or on individuals in your target market. When you have the answers, you will know where to go with your marketing – which groups to target for membership or speaking opportunities, which publications to pitch for articles, which events to attend, etc.

The client profile will help you to focus your marketing efforts, plan effective means of reaching your ideal clients, and develop methods to serve them better. The insight it provides can be invaluable for the future of your practice. But don't create your ideal client profile and then put it away. It is important to revisit it regularly to keep it up to date.

BUILDING & MARKETING YOUR WEBSITE

By Gyi Tsakalaki

As an attorney (licensed in MI, not practicing), Gyi Tsakalakis is familiar with the unique considerations of marketing a law practice both effectively and ethically. In 2008, he founded AttorneySync, an online legal marketing agency, to help lawyers earn meaningful attention online because that's where clients are looking.

CHAPTER 8

Building & Marketing
Your Website

By Gyi Tsakalakis

In this chapter, we will discuss creating and marketing a law firm website. Our focus will be providing simplified and tactical solutions for getting online and earning meaningful traffic. This is by no means a comprehensive guide to internet marketing. We have intentionally kept things simple so that even technically unsophisticated lawyers can launch a site.

UNIQUE VALUE (SELLING) PROPOSITION

Before you do anything online, you need to spend some time considering the benefit of your services, how you solve your client's issues, and what distinguishes you from the lawyer down the street.

You need to be able to communicate the value of your services quickly in a way that is obvious to your intended potential clients.

Brainstorm answers to the following questions:

- Who is your target client? What characteristics do they share?
- What problems do they face? What demographic and psychographic information can you compile about them?
- What problems do you understand uniquely well? What solution can you deliver uniquely well?
- What are the true benefits you provide to your clients?
- What makes your offering unique and different?

Put yourself in your target client's shoes. If you have existing clients already, ask them why they chose you over your competitors. Ask friends and family to describe what they think you do and how you help your clients. Too many lawyers struggle to articulate what services they provide in terms that their prospective clients can easily and quickly understand. Your website will need to communicate the value of your services in a matter of seconds.

BUILDING A WEBSITE

Most modern-day clients will expect to be able to find information about you and your firm online. One of the places they will expect to find information is your website. While effective websites play an important role in demonstrating a lawyer's knowledge, skill, and experience, poorly designed and developed websites can actually hurt credibility with a prospective client.

Building an effective website can be achieved in a variety of ways. I'm going to focus on one specific way that balances simplicity, costs, and functionality.

The first step in creating a new website is research. Hopefully, you have already spent some time contemplating your unique selling proposition. If one of the purposes of your website is to attract new clients, you should spend some time thinking about who these people are and how you are uniquely positioned to serve them. Remember, your law firm website isn't for you. While you should be proud of your web presence, it should not be designed for you, but instead, for the people you want to attract as clients.

Once you have a good understanding of who your target audience is and what information your website ought to communicate to them, you can begin the building process which can be broken down into three distinct parts:

1. Domain Registration
2. Content Management System
3. Hosting

I encourage you to choose a domain that is easy to remember and reflects your practice. Here are some additional tips for choosing a domain:

- Use a .com extension.
- Avoid hyphens.
- Shorter is better.
- Include keywords descriptive of your practice.

Don't select an excessively long domain because you think you need to include your city, practice areas, and name in it. Instead, try to find a way to creatively include some practice-specific words.

Once you have selected a domain that is available, register it. You can really choose any domain registrar you want. However, I typically use Godaddy.com and Google Domains (https://domains.google/).

After domain registration, assuming you're not hand-coding your pages, you will need to choose a content management system (CMS). A CMS is basically website administration software. At the risk of great oversimplification, there are really two major options here:

- Proprietary Website Builders (e.g. Wix, Squarespace, etc.)
- Open Source (e.g. WordPress, Joomla, Ghost, etc.)

If you choose a proprietary CMS, you will likely have to pay a licensing fee to use the software. Further, the CMS will probably be bundled with hosting and have a very limited feature set when compared to an open source counterpart. However, proprietary website builders are usually a bit more user-friendly out of the box.

My recommendation is simple: **Just use WordPress.** Here's why:

- General Public License - You don't have to pay to use it.
- A global community of developers supports it.
- It is relatively easy to use.

Having worked with hundreds of law firms and most of the major website building tools, I can tell you rather confidently that WordPress will be your best choice. You can download the software from WordPress.org; however, many hosts provide single-click WordPress installation.

After you've registered a domain and chosen a CMS, you will need to create a hosting environment. Too many lawyers opt for the cheapest hosting they can find. This is a huge mistake that is likely to create a multitude of hosting problems in the future. Assuming you're working with WordPress, you should choose a managed WordPress host. Here are some of the best options:

- WPEngine (this is the one I recommend)
- SiteGround
- Pagely
- DreamHost
- LiquidWeb

Whichever host you choose, be sure that they are fast (research benchmarking studies on them), provide regular back-ups, are secure, and provide excellent support. On balance, we have found WPEngine, while a bit more expensive, provides the best balance of speed, security, and support.

Once you have registered a domain, pointed to your host, and installed WordPress, you are ready to add a theme and create pages.

There are three major types of themes: free, premium, and custom. There are a seemingly endless number of free WordPress themes available at WordPress.org. The main advantage of a free theme is that it's, well, free. If cost is your primary factor, you should choose a well-supported, responsive free theme.

With premium themes, you pay a one-time licensing fee to use the theme. Generally speaking, the fee will be less than one-hundred dollars. I typically recommend premium themes. They usually provide the best balance in terms of cost, support, and functionality.

Finally, if you want a completely unique theme built specifically for you, you can commission the design and development of a custom WordPress site. A completely custom theme can run in the thousands of dollars.

Regardless of which theme option you choose, make sure your theme is well-supported (developers are regularly releasing updates), secure (doesn't expose your site to hacks), and responsive (layout adjusts to the environment, i.e., desktop, tablet, and mobile). Once you've installed your theme, you are ready to create pages and posts.

EARNING TRAFFIC TO A WEBSITE

Once you've launched your website, it is time to start earning traffic. This is where the real work begins. First, it's important to understand a few common types of traffic:

- **Direct** - A catch-all bucket for traffic that can't be identified (includes type-in traffic, bookmarked traffic, etc.)

- **Organic Search** - Traffic from clicks on organic listings in major search engines (i.e., Google, Bing, etc.).

- **Paid Search** – Traffic from clicks on paid search ads (i.e., AdWords, paid Bing listings, etc.)

- **Referral Traffic** - Traffic from other websites (i.e., legal directories, editorial links from other sites to your site, etc.)

- **Social traffic** - Traffic from major social networking platforms (i.e., Facebook, LinkedIn, Twitter, etc.)

A healthy, well-marketed website will have a diverse traffic profile. In other words, it will earn traffic from a variety of sources. Too many lawyers become too reliant on traffic from too few sources. This makes them vulnerable to changes in search engines and social networks.

Perhaps the most straightforward way to earn traffic is to publish a blog. **Traffic from blogging generally works as follows:**

1. You publish a post.
2. You get it in front of the right people.
3. Those people like it, link to it, and share it.
4. Users of search engines find it.
5. People subscribe to be notified when you publish new posts.
6. People click on links from other sites that have linked to your posts.

Blogging can be a fantastic way to generate traffic. However, effective blogging requires time and skill. Don't assume that simply because you post something, people will want to read it and come back to read more.

SEARCH ENGINE OPTIMIZATION

Search engine optimization (SEO) involves everything you can do to improve the quantity and quality of traffic your pages receive from people who click on organic search results.

While most major search engines use hundreds of factors to rank pages, we can group these into two major sets of factors:

- **On-Page Factors** - Everything you can do to your pages to improve their visibility in search results.
- **Off-Page Factors** - Everything you can do "around the web" to improve your pages' visibility in search results.

With respect to on-page factors, here are a few of the most important:

- **URL Structure** - Prefer unique, descriptive URLs that humans can read.
- **Title Tags** - Prefer unique, concise, and compelling page titles.
- **Meta Descriptions** - Prefer unique and compelling meta descriptions.
- **Headings** - Use only one, unique H1 tag per page.
- **Page Speed** - Make sure your pages load in around one second.
- **TSL** - Implement TSL (SSL, HTTPS, etc.) protocol to secure your pages.

- **Mobile-Friendly** - Make sure your pages render properly on mobile devices (probably by using a responsive design).

When we discuss off-page factors, for the most part, we're talking about links from other pages around the web that point to your pages. Generally speaking, links to a page count as votes for that page in the eyes of search engines. However, not all link-votes are given the same weight. Links from highly relevant and popular pages are given much more weight than those from unrelated and unpopular pages.

For example, if we are marketing our criminal defense firm's pages, a link from the homepage of The National Association of Criminal Defense Lawyers (NACDL) website (https://www.nacdl.org) will carry much more weight than a link from a relatively obscure blogger who seldom writes about criminal legal issues.

Here's a quick checklist for creating new pages to generate targeted organic search traffic:

Google | how to find the best family

how to find the best family **law attorney**
how to find the best family **doctor**
how to find the best family **counselor**
how to find the best family **cell phone plan**

Press Enter to search

1. Research search queries that are relevant and for which there is likely traffic. Use Google autocomplete, "people also ask" results, and related searches.
2. Create a new page that provides information relevant to the query. Be sure to include relevant keywords in the page's URL, title, meta description, and heading tag.
3. Identify sites around the web that might be interested in linking to or sharing your pages.
4. Find ways to motivate other site owners to help publicize your pages.

If you use WordPress, you should consider installing and configuring Yoast's WordPress SEO plugin. This will help guide you through the most important on-page SEO factors.

LOCAL SEO

Local SEO includes everything you can do to rank in "local search results." Local search results can be:

- Traditional organic results with local intent (i.e., Chicago criminal defense attorney)
- Map pack and Google maps results

With respect to local SEO factors, Google has provided the following:

- Relevance - How well a local listing matches what someone is searching for.
- Distance - How far each search result is from where the searcher is looking.
- Prominence - How well-known a business is.

Here are a few tips for ranking in local search engine results. First, verify your Google My Business listing. Be sure to add as much information to your listing as possible, including photos, hours of operation, correct categorization, your address, and local phone number.

Second, make sure your firm's Name, Address, and local Phone number (NAP) appear consistently on your site. I tend to recommend including this information on every page of a firm's site in the footer.

Third, make sure your firm's NAP information appears consistently across the web. This should include legal directory listings, social networking sites, author bylines on sites to which you contribute, professional organization profiles, and local business directories.

Once you have the basics down, most of your time should be spent working on your firm's prominence. To improve prominence, focus on earning online testimonials, earning links from local websites, and creating pages for relevant local topics.

PAID SEARCH ADVERTISING

With paid search advertising, advertisers pay search engines for listings. The most popular paid search advertising platform is Google's AdWords. While Google makes advertising with AdWords very simple, getting a return on your AdWords media spendings can be challenging.

If you're inclined to manage your own AdWords campaigns, you ought to spend significant time learning how AdWords works and how you will measure success. Here are some basic tips for maximizing your success with AdWords:

- Prefer exact and phrase match keywords over the broad match.
- Make sure there is a high degree of relevance between your keyword bids, ad copy, and landing pages.
- Where appropriate include as many relevant ad extensions as you can.
- Stick to search ads only and opt-out of the Google Display Network.
- Limit your ad schedule to times where a human being answers your firm's phone.
- Limit your ad geography to directly around your office and only in states, counties, and cities in which you will take clients. Keep in mind that for many searchers, your proximity to their location will play a significant role in their likelihood of contacting and hiring you.

Most lawyers don't have the time and experience needed to successfully create, manage, and optimize paid search campaigns. Therefore, it usually makes sense to talk to a seasoned paid search management agency with experience advertising law practices.

CONVERSION

Traffic is only valuable if it eventually converts into paying clients. However, before traffic can become an actual paying client, the visitor will likely need to first become a potential client inquiry. Here are the most common ways that visitor traffic will convert into a potential client inquiry:

- Phone call (still the most common way potential clients engage lawyers)

- Email / form (potential client submits a message through a website)
- Live chat (potential client initiates a live chat dialogue on a website)

Motivating site visitors to convert is both art and science. At its core, conversion rate optimization (CRO) involves testing a variety of website content, offers, calls to action, and methods of interaction. Different messaging is likely to appeal to different members of your target audience.

MEASUREMENT

Finally, the only way to improve the performance of your firm's web presence is through measurement. Fortunately, the web is built for this. The key is determining what metrics actually have meaning. Here are a few suggestions:

- Return on Investment (ROI) - Ideally, you are able to measure the actual value in fees of time and money you spend online.
- Return on Ad Spend (ROAS) - This is a specific evaluation of fees generated from a particular online advertising campaign.
- Cost Per Client - Hopefully, you've defined a target cost per client in the context of what the value of a client is to your firm in fees.
- Cost Per Inquiry (Lead) - If you are unable to determine a target cost per client, you may decide to focus on a cost per inquiry (i.e., how much money you can spend to generate a potential client inquiry).
- Traffic by Source - While traffic alone won't pay your bills, it can be a decent indirect metric of the effectiveness of your online activities. At a minimum, you should measure increases in traffic by source (i.e., organic, paid search, social, etc.).

At a minimum, you should use Google Analytics & Search Console. Google Analytics provides information about how people are finding your web pages and what they are doing once they arrive on your site. Search Console (formerly Webmaster Tools) provides information about how Google "sees" your site. This is one of the best interfaces we have for identifying issues with our pages in the eyes of Google.

While critically important, Analytics and Search Console aren't sufficient for measuring from clicks to fees. In order to truly track metrics like ROI and ROAS, you will need to implement more sophisticated measurement systems, including:

- Dynamic Call Tracking - Phone call tracking software that includes calls by source (e.g., CallRail).
- Client Relationship Management - A tool that marries front-end marketing data (clicks and calls) to business data (clients and fees).

As you might imagine, there are many ways to implement these systems. If you do nothing else, install and configure Google Analytics and CallRail. This way, you will be able to track how potential clients arrived at your website and from where they are calling.

CHAPTER 9

HOW TO DEVELOP A SUCCESSFUL INTERNET ADVERTISING CAMPAIGN

By Jason Marsh

—

Jason is the founder of MARSH8, a digital marketing firm that specializes in new client acquisition and online marketing strategies for law firms. Jason is the Chair of the ABA Law Practice Division's Client Development & Marketing Committee.

CHAPTER 9

How to Develop a Successful Internet Advertising Campaign

By Jason Marsh

For as long as advertising has been around, and it's been a while, there's been a saying:

"Half the money I spend on advertising is wasted; the trouble is I don't know which half."

- John Wanamaker (1838-1922)

This quote refers to the feeling many advertisers using traditional ad media (print, radio, and television) had about the effectiveness of their advertising until the last fifteen years or so. Businesses knew that their advertising was working in general, but couldn't quite pinpoint the specific aspects of the ad campaigns that made them successful. However, that began to change in the early 2000's as the internet matured and new forms of internet-based advertising emerged.

THE 3 KEYS TO A SUCCESSFUL AD CAMPAIGN

Today's "digital advertising" channels offer three very important characteristics that drive the success and performance of any modern advertising campaign: targeting, measurability, and scalability.

TARGETING

Targeting means showing the right ad to the right person. After all, even a great ad shown to the wrong person = a waste of money. So, getting your ads in front of the right audience is always the first order of business. And digital advertising channels offer an unprecedented level of targeting in comparison to traditional ad mediums.

MEASURABILITY

Measurability is the key to determining what is working and what isn't. As the saying goes, "You can't manage what you can't measure." So, it is critical to be able to evaluate, in detail, how well ad campaigns are working, how specific components and different ads are performing, and what the return on investment (ROI) of the campaign is. Measurements provide insight into fundamental business metrics that will help with budgeting and decision-making. After all, marketing is an investment in your firm. And it MUST have a quantifiable return.

SCALABILITY

Lastly is scalability. Once we've identified a strong target audience and built a successful campaign to reach those people (as determined by the data), the next step is to expand the campaign to reach more of the same people and generate similar results at a similar cost ratio. The goal is to expand a marketing campaign with a proven model that delivers repeatable and predictable outcomes. Digital advertising makes this possible.

So, when we put these three unique digital marketing characteristics in today's marketing landscape, we can update that quote from 100 years ago to say something like this:

> **"Very little of the money I spend on advertising is wasted, and I know exactly what I'm getting out of it."**
>
> *- Digital Advertiser (2018)*

Advertising Objectives: Branding vs. Direct Response

Before we get into the specific channels available to digital advertisers, let's first talk about objectives.

All forms of advertising can be put into two buckets: branding and direct response. It's important to understand each of these principles because each plays a unique role in the overall marketing mix.

BRAND ADVERTISING

Many people think of branding as a logo or some colors. That's merely a small part. A brand is much bigger and more important than that. It is a level of awareness and perception that your target audience has about your practice in general and about the services you provide specifically.

The overarching goal is to be top of mind. If you're a personal injury attorney in Miami, and someone gets into a car accident, you should always be the first person they think of. If you live in South Florida, you've probably heard radio ads for one particular company that has a very catchy jingle to all of their ads that starts with, "Accident, crash, slip or fall, it's just one call." Because everyone hears their jingle ten times a day, they are always top of mind and will always be remembered in these specific situations.

BRANDING

When someone needs a [   ] lawyer, be the first firm they think of.

The goal of brand advertising is to positively influence customer or client perceptions and influence purchasing decisions. This is especially important in a commoditized market where buyers of legal services have a difficult time differentiating between the options available to them. In this type of scenario, brand advertising is a tool that promotes differentiation among competing offerings, and positions the individual lawyer or law firm as the better option. In short:

Be **THE** lawyer. Not just **A** lawyer.

Creating this belief (or feeling) about your firm is the fundamental goal of a brand advertising campaign. In sum, build awareness, increase the firm's visibility in the community or industry, cement a strong reputation, and position your firm as the leading provider.

It's not easy. But if you can successfully build your firm's brand and develop a purchasing preference among your target audience, the real magic of a powerful brand will emerge in the ability to charge higher fees. And charging more money for the same product or service is something every successful brand advertiser is keenly aware of.

DIRECT-RESPONSE ADVERTISING

The other form of advertising is known as direct response. This form of advertising is uniquely suited to the digital landscape and extremely effective.

The goal of direct response advertising is simple: drive the viewer of an ad to take a specific action. For example: call now, request a consultation, download this free eBook, request more information...

Online advertising comes in a variety of different forms (or channels, as we say in the industry). So, it is important to understand how they apply to the branding and direct response forms of advertising. The primary channels you must be aware of are:

- Paid Search
- Paid Social
- Banners
- Remarketing
- Directory

PAID SEARCH ADVERTISING

Paid search is likely the most important online advertising channel for law firms. It is dominated by Google and their advertising platform, Google AdWords.

The reason paid search advertising is so powerful is that it is "high intent."

Targeting is based on specific search queries (known as keywords) a Google user enters into the search box (e.g., "Orlando divorce lawyer"). This type of targeting is extremely effective simply because an advertiser can target an audience based on the user's self-identified need or intention. An individual types in exactly what they are looking for.

Advertisers are charged only when an individual clicks the ad. This is known as a pay-per-click or PPC advertising. The cost of each ad click is based on advertiser demand. This is determined by an auction-based platform where advertisers essentially "bid" on the maximum amount they are willing to pay for a single click of a specific keyword. In competitive practice areas (e.g., personal injury, criminal defense, etc.) clicks can become quite expensive. So, measuring the effectiveness of paid search campaigns is key.

Because of the high intent nature of paid search advertising, it is highly effective. However, this has made it a very popular (translate: expensive) advertising channel, as many attorneys are targeting (and competing for) the very same keywords.

That being said, paid search typically is the strongest performing online advertising channel for law firms. It carries the greatest potential to generate new business inquiries. But, it is important to note that the competitive landscape and resulting costs of advertising in paid search make it vital that the campaign is being effectively managed and measured to ensure ROI.

For those readers not clear on how paid search advertising works, here's a quick overview…

Google

orlando divorce attorney

Google Search   I'm Feeling Lucky

A Google Search user types what they are interested in, e.g.:

Google then returns a results page for that specific search query, with anything from one to four ads appearing at the top of the page...

Lastly, once you've setup your campaign in Google and have it performing well, consider copying the campaign over to Bing. This is fairly easy to do. And while Bing has far fewer users and traffic than Google, it also has less advertiser competition. So, there is an opportunity to generate traffic at a lower cost than Google. However, as always, be sure to carefully measure results to ensure the quality of traffic and that performance justifies the investment.

PAID SOCIAL ADVERTISING

The next online advertising channel to be aware of is paid social. This, very simply, is advertising within social networks like Facebook, Instagram, LinkedIn, and Twitter. For the most part, Facebook is the primary one you will want to focus on, but it entirely depends on the specific audience you are trying to reach and which channel provides the best vehicle to reach them.

Paid social advertising offers both direct response and branding potential. And while advertising on Facebook and other social media platforms are becoming increasingly popular, it is still a relatively inexpensive channel to market your firm. Campaigns can be run for as little as $5 per day.

When it comes to paid search advertising, the first step is identifying and targeting the right audience. That is the foundation of your advertising strategy. So, it is important to understand who your target audience is, and most importantly, who it is not.

Identifying Your Audience(s)

The foundation of your Facebook strategy is to understand *who* your target audience is...

When thinking about the people that you want to target, consider segmenting your audience into different groups, sometimes called profiles or "personas." Not everyone you're trying to reach is the same. It is important to break your audience into different groups so that you can craft unique messaging to appeal to each unique segment.

Identifying Your Audience(s)

Prospective Clients

Influencers
(Media, Professional Associations)

Legal Professionals

When thinking about the different types of audiences you might target, potential new clients are obviously key. But what about influencers within your community, practice area, or industry, such as bloggers, media, and non-legal industry professionals? Or other attorneys? Each of these can potentially be a source of new business. Raising the firm's awareness among these other groups can be valuable from a referral standpoint. Again, it is all about staying top-of-mind.

AD TARGETING ON FACEBOOK

Since we've established how important targeting is to a digital advertising strategy, let's review Facebook specifically, and some of the unique and powerful targeting options it offers.

CUSTOM AUDIENCES BASED ON WEBSITE TRAFFIC

Custom Audiences based on website traffic (also known more generally as remarketing or retargeting) target people who have already visited your website. This is generally the best audience to start with. It works by placing a small piece of code on all the pages of your website. Visitors to your website who also have a Facebook account will then be eligible to start seeing your ads.

This audience is powerful because the people in it have already touched your firm. They've visited your site. Based on that alone, there is an implicit interest in your firm. Whether an individual visited your site via an advertisement or was just searching Google, you now have the ability to continue messaging him or her to extend your messaging and highlight your firm's core values, as well as why they should hire you.

CUSTOM AUDIENCES BASED ON CUSTOMER DATA

Another very powerful targeting feature within Facebook is Customer Audiences. Here, you can upload existing client data (name, email address, phone number, mailing address, etc.), and Facebook will try to match the data with existing users. Note: ideally, you want to upload data for your best, happiest clients.

Building an advertising audience based on client data is powerful because it allows you and your firm to build your brand and continue to stay top of mind with existing and past clients. By staying in front of past clients and continuing to reinforce your core value proposition, you're much more likely to receive new referrals from them.

LOOKALIKE AUDIENCES

Earlier, we talked about the ability to scale a successful advertising campaign. Using the targeting methods discussed to this point, you may eventually find that you want to reach a wider audience of similar people. This is exactly what Lookalike Audiences are designed to do. Within Facebook, you can create an entirely new audience that "looks like" an existing audience (e.g., website audience or client data audience), especially one that has generated successful results.

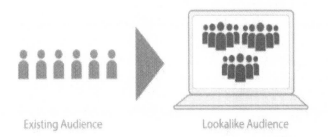

Existing Audience   Lookalike Audience

INTEREST AND DEMOGRAPHIC-BASED AUDIENCES

Given the amount of information that Facebook has on its users based on a wide variety of factors, advertisers have the opportunity to target individuals based on a similarly wide range of interest- and demographic-based criteria. While this method of audience targeting is worth some experimentation, it is worth noting that this is often the least effective targeting method of those mentioned previously. So, it is recommended to use this targeting method cautiously, and only to increase the reach and size of your campaign.

LEVERAGING CONTENT IN AD CAMPAIGNS TO SHOWCASE EXPERTISE

One great way to leverage Facebook advertising is to promote your knowledge and expertise with content. The primary goal of a content strategy is to enhance your reputation and build trust across your target audience. Facebook provides a wonderful vehicle to ensure your content reaches your audience on a regular basis.

For example, regardless of your practice area, consider offering free resources for relevant and valuable information that prospective clients would be interested in learning more about, such as eBooks, guides, or existing website content. In doing so, you position yourself as an "expert" and trusted resource.

While you can (and should) offer your content for free, you may also consider "gating" your content, meaning that if someone on your website wants your free eBook, they will need to provide their name and email in exchange. And for those who do, you can then add those prospects to your sales funnel via a mailing list or set of email autoresponders with the goal of nurturing that relationship over time.

MEASURING AD CAMPAIGNS AND INVESTING FOR SUCCESS

The key to a successful advertising campaign is carefully measuring the results to determine whether or not they are successful.

The entire goal of your advertising strategy is simple: return on investment (ROI).

As anyone who invests in anything (stocks, bonds, real estate, etc.) knows, there are often many different and competing investment opportunities. The same goes for digital advertising. There are many different channels, ad units, and the like. It is important to understand the potential and actual return of each so that, theoretically, limited investment dollars can be directed to the highest performing channels to deliver the maximum return on investment.

One of the most important benefits of online advertising is the incredible amount of data which is available. This data enables advertisers' great precision in measuring and managing campaigns, with a particular emphasis on ROI.

Put simply, ROI is the calculation of the difference between how much money was spent on the campaign and how much revenue (or income) the campaign generated. So, if you invested $10,000 in the campaign and generated $20,000 in revenue, the return on investment is $10,000, or 100%.

Let's get more detailed with how we think about the numbers, though. The first step is considering the relative value of a single client or matter to the firm. In other words, how much money, on average, is a new client worth to the firm? In most cases, there will be a range. But it is worth calculating a conservative average Lifetime Value (LTV) for the type of client you are interested in acquiring.

Once you have a reasonable idea of the LTV of a client, you can start thinking about client acquisition costs. That is the amount of money you will need to invest in acquiring these clients. This is often referred to as "cost of acquisition." And over time, cost of acquisition is a critical number to fully understand and be able to calculate by channel. In short, for each specific advertising channel you are investing in, what does it cost to generate a new client?

Another important and slightly simpler way to evaluate your advertising channels is by cost per lead. Simply put, how much does it cost to generate a new phone call, web form inquiry, or live chat in a given advertising channel? While this is a quick way to assess the cost of generating new client inquiries, it does not account for the quality or ultimate result of the inquiries. So, determining the average quality of the leads produced by a given channel is an additional factor that will need to be considered.

THE ADVERTISING INVESTMENT MATH

Some basic math or accounting will be required when calculating the value of a new client, the cost of acquiring that new client, and ultimately the return on investment.

In the top part of the following chart, we are assuming that a new client is worth $10,000 in new revenue to the firm over the life of the relationship.

(It is worth noting that the LTV number itself does not matter in this calculation. It can be $1,000 or $100,000. It is the overall concept and percentages which matter to the calculation.) Assuming a traditional service-based business model that fits for many law firms (and your numbers may vary) we are assuming direct labor costs to deliver legal services of 50% and overhead costs of 25%. Lastly, in our calculation, we entered $1200 (or 12%) as a possible client acquisition cost number.

Avg. Value of Client (LTV)	$10,000
Direct Costs (Labor)	50%
Indirect Costs (Overhead)	25%
Client Acquisition Cost	**$1,200**
REVENUE	**$10,000**
Direct Costs	$5,000
Indirect Costs	$2,500
Profit	**$2,500**
Your Client Acquisition Cost	$1,200
NET PROFIT	**$1,300**
Return on Investment	108%

What follows in the bottom part of the chart is the result of our calculations. In this specific case, on new revenue of $10,000 – after accounting for labor costs (if you are a solo or small firm, this is what you pay yourself) and associated overhead of servicing the matter – a gross profit of $2,500 was earned, translating to a net profit to the firm of $1,300, and a 108% return on investment.

When was the last time you had an investment generate a return close to or exceeding 100% in a relatively short time? If you're like most, probably not ever. But the most important thing about this investment is that it is your business, your law practice, which means you control a great deal of the risk equation.

So, the question becomes, do you have a clear investment strategy for your business, and what does it look like?

SCALING FOR GROWTH

To this point, we've talked about the significance of targeting and measurability in online advertising as key drivers in what makes the medium so powerful. The last piece of the overall equation is scalability. It is the idea of taking what works and expanding it into a larger, repeatable, and profitable model.

So, looking at the mathematical equation previously, that represents just one single client. However, that's hardly the goal. The objective is to replicate those numbers on a much greater scale. So, let's say you could scale that model by 20X a year (or even a month), here's what it would look like:

$10,000 (LTV) IDEAL CLIENT X 20 (A YEAR, A MONTH?)

	(Per Client)	(20 Clients)
Avg. Value of Client (LTV)	$10,000	$200,000
Direct Costs (Labor)	50%	50%
Indirect Costs (Overhead)	25%	25%
Client Acquisition Cost	**$1,200**	**$24,000**
REVENUE	**$10,000**	**$200,000**
Direct Costs	$5,000	$100,000
Indirect Costs	$2,500	$50,000
Profit	**$2,500**	**$50,000**
Your Client Acquisition Cost	$1,200	$24,000
NET PROFIT	**$1,300**	**$26,000**
Return on Investment	108%	108%

The idea is not to generate a new one-off client here and there, but rather forming a profitable marketing program that can be repeated and scaled in a sustainable way to grow your practice. And digital advertising continues to prove to be a very reliable investment vehicle to do so.

Businesses (legal or otherwise) with evolved digital advertising programs have a clear picture of the effectiveness of their online ad campaigns. They know, with a high degree of reliability, that if they invest a dollar, how many new dollars with come out the other side.

BRANDING BOOTCAMP 101

By Nicole Abboud

Nicole Abboud is the Founder at Abboud Media - a video branding agency for lawyers. She is a Millennial speaker, producer and host of The Gen Why Lawyer Podcast, attorney, and college professor.

CHAPTER 10

Branding Bootcamp 101

By Nicole Abboud

Personal branding has been a huge part of my success as a business owner, podcaster, and lawyer. Taking the time to build a strong personal brand is one of the best ways to create a career and life you love. Really, it's one of the wisest investments you can make in yourself, in your business, and in your career. Speaking from personal experience, when I started focusing my energy and efforts on building my personal brand, more and more opportunities started presenting themselves.

Let's start from the top: what is a personal brand? As I see it, your personal brand is you, authentically-packaged and strategically presented to others in a way that makes you the go-to person in your practice area, business, or expertise.

You can think of personal branding as the sum of all experiences that people have when they interact with you. When others meet you, how do you leave them feeling? What emotions do you conjure up in people when they think about you or hear your name mentioned? Your personal brand is the effect that your interactions have on others.

I also like to think of your personal brand as a promise. It's a promise that each lawyer makes to their clients. It's also a promise that they make to the profession and to their community. This promise is what they stand for, what their value will be, and what they have to offer others.

In order to make better sense of this balancing act, we will go through a formula that breaks down personal branding:

Vision + Values + Value + Voice = Your Personal Brand

I don't know if there are any lawyers who actually love math, but that is what it would look like if we were to represent a personal brand as a formula. It follows, then, that the act of personal branding is the process of developing a strategy and intentional actions that shape your personal brand.

The journey of personal branding is a constant balancing act between exploring what you want out of life, and, making sure that you're serving those whom you want to serve (e.g., potential clients or members of the community). Take the time to really think about what you want out of your life and your career. Where do you see yourself in X number of years? How can you help others around you? What do you want to offer your clients and how do you want them to feel when they think about you?

We will explore these four V's further later into the chapter, but here is an overview of what each stand for:

- Your **Vision** is the grand picture of what you want to accomplish on this earth. What are you hoping to achieve in your lifetime?
- Your **Values** are the driving forces in your life.
- Your **Value** is your unique skill, talent, expertise, and/or experience. This is what we call your unique selling proposition. Again, we will delve deeper into this later in the chapter.
- Your **Voice** is how you communicate your value in order to make your vision come true.

Before I go any further, let me spend a moment on what a personal brand is not. Many people assume that their brand is merely their product, their logo, the colors on their website, the look and feel of their business cards, etc., but these are all simply small aspects of their overall personal brand. Many people mistakenly believe that personal branding is about bragging or self-promotion. That too is not personal branding.

Branding is more about that intangible feeling that you leave people with. It is the hard-to-describe-feeling that separates one lawyer from another. It is the underlying foundation that sets the tone for all marketing efforts. One's personal brand is what defines who they are as a person, as a lawyer, and as a community member.

Therefore, you can think of the process of personal branding as education management. It is helping people understand who you are, what you do, and who you serve. Thus, thinking about and working on your personal brand development and management is a critical element of your business and your career development.

So, why is building a personal brand so important to lawyers?

Regardless of whether or not you are fresh out of law school or have an established practice, people are naturally going to form opinions about you without even meeting you. This is something lawyers have to deal with constantly. We can choose to let that reputation be formed for us, or, we can take an active part in its formation and communication by establishing a brand for ourselves.

Personal branding is also important because there are over a million lawyers in the U.S. There is a lot of competition out there, so the need for a personal brand that stands out becomes all the more important in helping set one lawyer apart from another.

Most importantly, when you're faced with an important decision – like whether or not to take on a particular client or where to spend your marketing dollars – personal branding will help guide your decision making.

Lawyers who take the time to build a personal brand have an advantage in this competitive profession. A well-defined brand allows people to know who you are and what you're good at.

Nowadays it is easy for potential clients to jump online and search through a sea of lawyers. Thus, if you can stand out as the most helpful and most attractive for their specific needs, you're going to be ahead of the game. Crafting your personal brand will allow you to do that.

Before we move on to the formula, keep in mind that building your brand is going to be something that you're going to do for the rest of your life. Personal branding is not a set-it-and-forget-it system. It is something you're always going to have to work on because you are going to constantly evolve, as a lawyer and as a person. So, it only makes sense that your personal brand is going to evolve and grow with you.

ASSEMBLING YOUR PERSONAL BRAND

VISION

Vision is the beginning of any personal branding journey. Here, you get to take a step back and look at the big picture. Take some time to internalize what you want out of life and figure out where you want to go.

It can be difficult to predict where our lives are going to take us and where we are going to be in exactly ten or twenty years. That's not what I'm asking you to do. I'm asking you to dream big, without any inhibitions. Think of the greatest position you'd like to see yourself in in the future. What is your ultimate goal? Do you want to become a partner at your law firm? Do you want to transition out of the practice of law? Do you want to become a best-selling author? Do you want to start a non-profit organization? Your vision is the thing you want to work towards. By visualizing and outlining your vision, you will know where you need to start.

Keep in mind that the answers to the above questions won't be formed in a day. What you want out of life is going to change and evolve as you grow, but it is important to at least visualize some goals for yourself. These goals guide you in dissecting the steps that are necessary to get you there. In other words, the vision is the big picture, and the goals are the steps you need to take (daily, weekly, monthly, yearly) to get there.

So how do you figure out what you want? Here are some questions to help:

1. What do you want to accomplish in this world?
2. What do you want to be known for?
3. Where do you see yourself at the end of your career?
4. What is the ultimate end game for you?
5. What would you do if you weren't afraid to fail?
6. What would the ideal version of yourself be doing if you could do exactly what you wanted to do?

Again, setting goals will help you work towards your vision. These are the things that you need to set into motion to get you to where you want to be. Who do you need to meet with? Do you need a mentor? Do you need to change your practice area? Do you need to take an additional class to learn a new skill?

There are also different types of goals that you're going to set for yourself:

- Personal
- Professional
- Financial
- Long-term
- Short-term

Your personal goals are the ones that pertain to your daily activities like your health, well-being, finances, friends, and family.

Do you want to work sixty hours a week, or thirty hours a week, or how many? If you only want to work thirty, then what do you need to do to ensure that your work is done within that time frame? Do you need to hire an assistant? Do you need to cut down on your caseload?

Do want to travel more? Alright, how are you going to do that? Are you physically tied down to your office/location? Do you have someone competent and who you can trust to handle your affairs while you're away?

Do you want to have a family, and if so, how big of a family do you want? Do you want to be a stay-at-home parent? Are you okay with missing a few soccer games, or do you want to be there for every game?

These are just a few of the things you should think about beforehand so you can shape your vision.

Professional goals are anything that relates to your career. Do you want to open your own practice? Do you want to work for a big law firm? Do you want to transition into a different career?

Write down the answers to these questions and use strong descriptors and adjectives, because the more vivid you can make it, the more likely it is you'll attain it.

VALUES

Let us move on to values, the second "V" in the formula. Your values are the principles which guide and ground your life. I guess you can say they are the driving forces in your decision-making and your action-taking.

Understand that your core values are important when you're crafting your personal brand, because your values will inform your branding choices and will guide your day-to-day decisions, such as which jobs to apply for and which clients to take on. When you are faced with decisions, you should reassess and reaffirm your values before evaluating whether a certain decision is in alignment with who you are.

Some common values that people hold include hard work, dependability, honesty, community, collaboration, and diversity. Maybe something that is very valuable to you is security, honesty, belonging, or a sense of fairness. Identifying your values is important, because when you are faced with a decision – like whether or not you should apply to work for a certain firm – you're going to check to see if the firm's mission is in alignment with your values. If the firm is lacking in diversity, for example, and that's very important to you, then you will immediately know that it's not the right firm for you. This is all part of your brand. It is what you stand for; so the key to creating a successful personal brand is to identify your values.

VALUE

The third "V" is value, and this is hardest one for most people to pinpoint. Your value is your unique selling proposition ("USP"). This is what sets you apart from all other lawyers who are similarly situated. Your USP is something that only you possess – a skill, expertise, talent, experience, personality trait – that you can capitalize on as part of your personal brand.

Whether you have a background in computers, you speak a different language, you have insight into an industry like fashion or flash mobs, or you used to live on a farm and have in-depth knowledge of cattle, identify that special something about yourself and use it to your advantage. Use that USP to elevate yourself above the other lawyers who don't have such knowledge.

Some questions to ask yourself when you're trying to figure out what your value is:

- What personal characteristics set you apart from others?
- What life experiences have you had that make you best situated to offer your product or service?
- What special skills, talents, or knowledge do you possess?
- What is one skill that you possess that regularly receives compliments/ attention from others?
- Have you received advanced training in any particular subject?
- What do your friends and family members call upon you to help them with the most?
- What is your greatest strength?

VOICE

The fourth "V" in the branding formula is voice, and this is where the rubber meets the road. Now that you have an idea of what your goals, values, and strengths are, is it is time to actually get down to work. It is time to start speaking up and sharing your voice. Your voice is how you're going to communicate what your value is in order to make your vision come true. Your voice is how you're going to generate buzz for yourself and how you're going to establish yourself as a thought leader and authority in your space.

A big part of building a personal brand involves establishing yourself as the go-to lawyer in your practice area. In order to do that, you must establish yourself as an authority first. Being an authority, or thought leader, means being the one person whom others respect because of the depth of knowledge one has about a certain subject and whom others trust. This is what you want to strive for. You want to be that thought leader in your practice area.

How are you going to establish your thought leadership? Through content creation. This involves using any number of available platforms, both online and in-person. Writing blog posts, authoring articles, recording legal how-to videos, recording a podcast, hosting webinars, conducting seminars, live streaming, and posting on social media are all forms of content creation.

By engaging in any of these efforts, you're able to showcase what you know. Better yet, you're able to help prospective clients who read / listen to / watch your content. In doing so, you'll begin to create the perception that you are knowledgeable and helpful. That, in turn, builds the know, like, and trust factor. It is precisely that feeling of knowing someone, liking them, and trusting them that forms the foundation of an irresistible personal brand because prospective clients want to hire an attorney they trust and whom they believe is knowledgeable in their practice area.

It is important to note that a huge part of creating content is promoting your content and engaging with community members. After all, what good is your personal brand if there's no one on the other end benefitting from all your efforts? Thus, as you build your brand, always remember to build relationships with other like-minded individuals. Focus on building a community of people who support you and your efforts. These community members will be your cheerleaders and will help elevate your personal brand. Even though personal branding is a very personal journey, it's important to take others along for the ride.

A FINAL THOUGHT
Once you finish this chapter (and this entire book), I encourage you to think about what you want for your life and your career. Be as audacious as you want to be. No one is judging you, so write it down and think big. Start writing down the tiny steps necessary to reach your goals.

Also, it is one thing to merely think about your brand and another thing altogether to actually take action. When you start building your personal brand, you will notice amazing things happening. Not only will you gain control of your life and career, but you will begin attracting the right opportunities and making the right connections.

Nowadays, it is extremely important to put yourself out there. This is the new standard for marketing. Cultivating an attractive and solid personal brand will take you far in life. The sooner you begin working on your four V's, the sooner you can begin living the life you want.

BUSINESS DEVELOPMENT BEST PRACTICES

By Steve Fretzin

Driven, focused and passionate about helping attorneys reach their full potential, Steve Fretzin is regarded as the premier business coach, speaker and author on business development for attorneys.

CHAPTER 11

Business Development Best Practices

By Steve Fretzin

What Can a Lawyer Learn About Business Development from a Golf Pro?

I have played many rounds of golf over the past thirty years and have never put much thought into anything else but keeping the ball somewhere in-bounds. I was too busy swinging away, just trying to get to the next tee box without losing my ball. A few years ago, I met a golf instructor and decided to take a few lessons. It was a good thing I did, because it not only improved my game, bu it also provided a supplementary experience that really struck a chord with me as it related to business development.

As an attorney, you've probably been involved in a "pitch" meeting with a new prospective client. You may recall the nervousness or anxiety you felt about the importance of signing up this new business. During your meeting, you probably believed that the end result, or "close," is the single most important element of the meeting. While your origination numbers may depend on "closing the deal," there is another important aspect to running a successful business development meeting that holds the key to your success. Let me go back to my golf pro for a minute and explain.

After meeting and chatting with my new golf pro for a few minutes, he invited me onto the green carpet to take a few swings. He watched me intently for a few minutes as I stepped up and smashed a few balls into the range. Finally, he turned to me and said, "Steve, do you enjoy swinging the golf club?" Being terribly confused by his question, I said, "What?" I simply had no idea what he was talking about. He explained. "You seem to be approaching each swing with the intention of getting to the outcome as fast as possible. You don't seem to be enjoying the actual swing."

I paused and thought about that for a minute. Do I really enjoy swinging a golf club? Or am I just trying to get it over with, hoping to land the ball somewhere in-bounds? I slowly realized there was very little enjoyment in swinging the golf club, and I was in fact rushing each shot to quickly get to an outcome. For me, this conversation was a real epiphany. If the sport of golf is all about swinging a golf club repeatedly, and I am not enjoying the swing, then am I really enjoying the game of golf? Pretty deep, right?

At the time, I didn't have the skill-sets to truly enjoy the swing. Therefore, I was only focused on the end result of each shot. The true enjoyment of golf is in the beauty and enjoyment of each swing. It then became clear to me that a better, more fluid swing would produce a much better outcome. This is where the missing piece of the puzzle was for me. It's also where I realized how perfectly this scenario relates to attorneys and the process of business development.

As I thought more about the swing in golf and what happens in a typical pitch meeting, there was something unnatural about both of these activities. Just like my wild and harried swing, rushing to pitch a new prospective client can lead to an unpredictable outcome. A better solution would be to slow things down and enjoy conducting a successful business meeting. Instead of rushing to pitch and talk about yourself, focus on talking about the potential client, building rapport and asking great questions. Simply listen to your prospective client's legal problems without feeling obligated to solve them on the spot. While this might go against one's natural instincts to problem solve, it will be a refreshing change to focus on not solving problems. By concentrating on asking tough questions and uncovering a prospective client's pain points, there will be more urgency for them to hire you.

The "enjoyment of the swing" in business development is to be found in the relationship building and questioning process that allows us to truly understand our prospective client's problems, needs, and desires. If you focus your time and attention there, they are much more likely to believe that you are indeed an expert and someone with whom they should be working. Having your focus on the prospective client and not on yourself can only help you in developing a new client opportunity. It might also separate you from the other attorneys who are still hacking away with their salesy pitches.

Shift the focus to the buyer to achieve good results. Walk a buyer through a buying decision and enjoy your business development efforts. Take away the pressure to just "close the sale."

Effective Time Management for Lawyers: Is it Really Possible?

There seems to be never enough time left for lawyers to really think about, much less to engage in, business development and marketing activities. As a coach focusing solely on attorneys, I understand the stress and demands regularly faced by legal practitioners. I find myself spending a lot of time considering the demands being placed on a lawyer's time. Then, stress builds up as I discuss the time investment needed in business development. Given all this, it's no wonder most attorneys skip their marketing activities.

Time challenges aside, you must know by now that nothing will have a greater impact on your personal and financial freedom than having your own book of business. A book of business can be defined as a list of leads and clientele you can count on. When you have an address book, contact list in Outlook, an email list collected over the years, or many happy clients, you don't need to constantly be prospecting for new business, you can hopefully rely on them for future revenue.

Therefore, it's never been more important to effectively manage your time to ensure you can fit in the billable hours and business development. By the way, it sure would be nice to see your family too! Here are three tips to help you improve the balance in your practice to create the career you've been dreaming of:

Time Tip #1: Have a solid plan for business development.
Other than doing nothing, the worst thing you can do as a lawyer is to

approach business development in a haphazard fashion. Attending events, writing articles, or even speaking can be ineffective if your audience isn't aligned with your goals. You need to have a plan in writing to ensure you are spending your time in the right places with the right people. Think about the types of legal buyers and strategic partners you need to meet. Ask yourself: Where do they spend their time? How do I get in front of them? How many do I need to build relationships with to really grow my list of clients?

A good plan should lay out your goals, strategies, and tactics to accomplish your objectives in the fastest time possible. Think of the plan as a GPS for your car. Before we had this tool, we would drive miles out of our way before turning around or, heaven forbid, asking for directions. Now the GPS tells us immediately when we have made a wrong turn and how to get back on track. This is what a good plan will do for you.

Time Tip #2: Use your calendar to schedule time for business development.

You schedule your time for a closing, deposition, or a trial, then why not schedule time for business development? All are important and need to get done, so treat them with equal importance. Based on where you are in your career, how much time do you need to carve out to grow your book of business? There needs to be an emphasis on carving out time daily or weekly for business development. Here are a couple of thoughts and best practices to think about:

- Look at your calendar to find times when you are less likely to be distracted by email, phone calls, or other people in your office. Not to boast, but I get into my office three days a week at 6 a.m. This gives me a solid six hours a week when I can get emails out, leave voicemails, or make contacts through LinkedIn. If you're a night owl, after hours might be better for you.
- Once you do get meetings on your calendar, be sure to use the meeting invite tool to ensure that these meetings stick. Changing schedules and cancellations are sometimes inevitable; however, we can curtail that slightly by getting into someone's calendar right away. If you're not sure how to use this tool, ask the person in the office next to you. It's become as popular as emailing.

- Use your calendar to schedule EVERYTHING! If you have to make a call, write an email, or follow up with someone, schedule it. As I mentioned earlier, you need to start treating your marketing activities the same way you treat the law. Think of your schedule like an advanced "to-do" list. The more you use your calendar to schedule things, the more you will actually do. Just seeing a follow-up call pop up on your screen will prompt you to follow through.

Time Tip #3: Always pick the low-hanging fruit first.

With all of the networking groups, associations, and coffee meetings to choose from, you may quickly find your time draining away. One of the first things I suggest to attorneys is to look closely at their network and find the easiest way to obtain new business. This might include meeting with existing clients to cross-sell, up-sell, or find quality introductions. There might also be some family or friends who are in power positions but haven't been properly tapped into yet. Whatever the situation, it's critical to leverage these contacts first.

A concern that you might have with this approach is the possibility of blowing the opportunity or disrupting the relationship. While this is always a remote possibility, here are some soft and gentle approaches that might ease your mind when venturing into uncharted territory:

Be curious. You're a lawyer, right? Use that as your excuse to ask a thousand questions about this person's business. Everyone has goals and challenges that they're more than happy to share with you. Just be a great listener and ask open-ended questions to uncover possible needs. Then it might be more natural to discuss your value or services. An example of this would be at a family function where you see Uncle Dan every year. He owns a $20 million website company. You can ask him, "What do you love about your business?" and "What types of challenges do you have running a company of that size?" Once you start Uncle Dan talking about his favorite subject, himself, and his business, you can keep asking deeper questions to identify a possible need or a question he might have for you on the legal side.

Ask for advice. In this scenario, you are looking to better understand the mindset of a business owner or GC as you are working to grow your own practice. Ask some great questions to obtain their advice and help. It's then possible that they might try to help you with your goals, make an intro to someone they know, or allow you to share your knowledge to help with a problem within their own company.

Look to obtain an introduction from an existing client. Look, you're good at what you do and your client is happy with your representation. In addition, you've invested time taking him/her to lunch, a game, golfing, etc. Maybe it's time to ask for a high-level introduction to someone in their network who might benefit from a similar experience.

It might make sense to schedule a lunch with your client, and before getting off the call say, "I'm looking forward to our lunch on Friday. I do have a favor to ask that would mean a lot to me. I know you are well connected and have been happy with my work. Would you be open to introducing me around to one or two of your business associates?" This type of question is permission based and should be received positively. The worst that can happen is that the client will say "no." The best thing can be an intro to a new client that could make your year! Plus, if the client does say "no," it should be a wake-up call that you might need to work on your relationship-building skills.

Use these time management tips to help you get your time under control. Organize and plan how much time you'll spend on your priorities. Set aside time on your calendar for business development, create a plan, and then focus on activities that will lead to new business.

The Legal Language of Business Development

Is it a challenge for you to ask for business from your existing relationships such as friends, family, or clients? If yes, you are one of many attorneys facing this challenge. Reasons for this typically include:

- Fear of rejection;
- The impression of being too "salesy"; or
- The mindset that you wouldn't want someone asking you for something.

Sound about right? This is the time to truly understand and use the legal language of business development to grow your book of business.

One of the best ways to get on track as it relates to growing your book of business is to focus on your best contacts and use some specific language to help you overcome the "head-trash" that you may be experiencing. Scripting out a few words before making a call like this may be the difference between obtaining five new clients this year or none at all. By the way, waiting for the phone to ring is not an effective or proactive strategy to growing your book this year.

Here are a few scripts that have been very successful for my clients to assist in obtaining new business from a friend, family member, referral source, and even an existing client. These scripts can be used to set up the meeting beforehand or during the meeting.

The key to success with these scripts is to:

- Make the script a part of the conversation.
- Make sure the script is used in a conversational manner.
- The script should be permission based.
- Be sure to adjust and adapt each script to your own personality and style.

Script #1 - A friend where you've never discussed business before:

"I was thinking that we haven't really had the opportunity to discuss our businesses with one another and it might be valuable to learn more about what each other does as new issues come across our desks. Would you be open to a lunch where we learn more about one another and see if there are synergies?"

Script #2 - A long-time family member where you've never discussed business before:

"I'd love the opportunity to grab a coffee or lunch with you in the next week or two. We see each other every year, but I still don't really know a great deal about what you do. I'd love to learn more about your business and see how I can be a

resource for you moving forward. I'd also enjoy sharing a little about what I do, as I know you run into people regularly with legal concerns. Are you free on... (provide specific dates)."

Script #3 - A lawyer or past referral source that you believe may have business for you:

"In addition to catching up next week when we meet for lunch, I'd like to share some possible contacts with you that might be beneficial to your business/practice. I've been really focused lately on helping people who have helped me in the past. I'd also like to pick your brain for ideas on contacts that might make sense for what I'm doing. Is that okay with you?"

Script #4 - A "happy" past or existing client who is well connected, but not currently offering you referrals:

"Before we meet on (date), I thought it might be helpful to think of some business connections that might be good for one another. As you know, I'm looking to meet (name a specific type of prospective client). If you're open to it, let's come up with a few names prior to meeting, that way we can both get more value from our time together."

OR

"I know you've been very happy with the work I've done over the past few years and I was thinking that you may know other business owners who would appreciate the high-level work I perform. Would you be open to discussing a few contacts with me when we meet for lunch next week? It would be really meaningful to me."

OR

"There's something I'd like to ask of you and it goes outside of my comfort zone a little, but it's important to me. I know how well connected you are and I was hoping that you'd be open to discussing some possible connections with me during our lunch next week. Is that something we can chat about?"

While there are many different ways to approach the people you know for introductions, my clients have found that success happens when you try the scripts and begin to see results from your efforts.

The proof of success can only be achieved through trying this approach a few times, and eventually getting introductions and leads. You will need to at least try to speak the legal language of business development by adapting these scripts. Doing this over time and having some success in it will build your confidence and make speaking the language of business development a natural transition.

CHAPTER 12

13 WAYS LAWYERS CAN REPURPOSE CONTENT ON SOCIAL MEDIA

By Mitch Jackson

—

Mitch Jackson enjoys combining law, social media and live streaming to disrupt, hack, and improve his clients' companies, causes, and professional relationships. He's an award-winning 2009 Orange County Trial Lawyer of the Year and 2013 California Litigation Lawyer of the Year, who enjoys speaking around the world about business, law and digital.

CHAPTER 12

13 Ways Lawyers Can Repurpose Content on Social Media

By Mitch Jackson

Social media is all about sharing good content and helping others. Top-of-mind awareness and results come from engaging, caring, and providing value. My general rule is that only 20% of my posts on the various platforms are about my firm or me. The other 80% are focused on sharing valuable tips, helping others, newsjacking, and curating good third-party content that I believe will be useful to my audience. This article is about the first 20%.

OVERVIEW

Something exciting has just happened and you want to share the good news with the world. You've just settled a big case or obtained a favorable verdict. Maybe you've even made new case law. Here are 13 ways to share this news with your "tribe" (former and current clients, family, friends, and other followers on social media).

Before we get started, remember that in today's digital world, we're all media companies. Having a digital presence is important. Producing, sharing good content, and engaging with others is mandatory to building your brand and to long-term success. It's also important to understand and appreciate the fact that while content is king, context is everything. Each platform is different (some more than others), so care must be taken to post and share the right way on each platform.

On a side note, in my blog post, "The Ultimate Social Media Success Blueprint for Lawyers" (found at LegalMinds.lawyer), I've shared in detail exactly how I setup and use the major social media platforms. This site is my private global mastermind group for lawyers and other professionals. If you have access to the post, feel free to review it as you make your way through this chapter.

Also, remember that learning and using social media is neither a sprint nor a marathon. There really is no finish line. I believe building a digital footprint on social media is more like working out and getting in shape. Because social media, consumer expectations, and human behavior is always changing, the digital dance is continuous and constantly changing. Be patient; never stop learning; take daily action; and a year from now you'll be far ahead of your competition.

Here's how I save a ton of time by doing the above and repurposing my social media content.

STEP #1: WEBSITE AND BLOG

Share your good news or update in a properly written blog post. Use effective headings and appropriate keywords. Use a story format and write in your own voice and in a non-legal way. Make the post interesting and easy to read. Increase interaction by always including a picture, graphic, or video.

If you're writing blog posts that look and sound like all the other lawyers out there, then you're doing things wrong. Be yourself and unique. Share your art.

If you don't have a website or blog, then get it done. This needs to be a high priority. Everyone and everything is going mobile (smartphones and tablets), so make sure your site is mobile responsive – no exceptions. I'm a big fan of WordPress blogs using Studio Press themes hosted on the new GoDaddy WordPress Hosted service or WPEngine. For those of you who are not DIY kind of peeps, a good third-party option is the attorney website service offered by my friend, Tom Foster, of FosterWebMarketing.com.

STEP #2: TWITTER

Share the catchy caption or heading of your blog post, together with a short descriptive sentence on Twitter. Include a link back to your post. Use a hashtag. Although Twitter allows for 140 characters, try and keep your post to about 120 characters to leave room for people to retweet with comments.

Pictures attract more attention. As such, add the picture you used in your post to your tweet. If you don't have a picture, use one of the free or paid online services to grab an image that relates to your story. I use Fotolia.com.

One of my favorite techniques is to download and use the free screenshot service called "Jing" by TechSmith to screenshot a picture at my blog post to use later for posting on the other social platforms.

While you're thinking about Twitter, take your blog post and break it down into five to ten 120-word "teasers" highlighting key points and topics contained within your blog. Each snapshot or tweet is worded in its own unique and eye-catching way. I use a Word or Google document and keep a list of these mini-snapshot tweets for future use.

Sit down at night or early in the morning and use Hootsuite or Buffer to schedule these additional tweets once or twice a day over the next five to thirty days. If you're short on time, you can use the "auto schedule" function to let the service pick the time and date of your scheduled tweets. Link each tweet back to your original blog post.

Instead of doing written tweets, you can instead shoot a quick video using the Twitter app about each topic of the short tweets. In most cases, a combination of the above is the best way to get your message heard by the largest audience possible.

Twitter Live (also see Periscope below)

This new live video component of Twitter allows you to hop on a live video and share your new post with your Twitter followers. Make sure to engage with your audience in the comments and share how your post will help them or solve a problem. Consistency is key with live video, and over time you'll build an audience who will share your live streams with their audience on Twitter.

STEP #3: LINKEDIN

Take one or more of the tweets that you have listed in your Word document and share them on LinkedIn, linking back to your blog post. Normally I do this in the above step by telling Hootsuite or Buffer to send out the tweets I schedule to both Twitter and LinkedIn (these apps let you easily do this).

STEP #4: FACEBOOK

Again, I take one or more of the tweets I've listed in my Word or Google document and repurpose the language for Facebook. Unlike Twitter, Facebook posts can be longer, so I usually add a bit more information in Word (or directly in the Facebook post) before posting on Facebook with the link back to my original blog post.

Images are powerful attention-grabbing magnets on Facebook and will result in more interaction, shares, and comments. Because of this, make sure to include an image with your post. Rather than allowing the link to my blog post to automatically pull an image back into my Facebook feed, I prefer to upload my own image from the blog post. Doing this will display a larger image in your Facebook post.

I have a personal as well as business Facebook profile, and depending on the nature of the content, I post to each once or twice a day. I also manage a couple of Facebook public and private Facebook groups, and if the content is relevant, I also may modify the post and share to the groups too. The key is to always think about how you can repurpose content more than once.

Facebook Live - This new live video option is huge, and you should embrace everything about it. Together with Twitter Live, aka Periscope, these new live streaming apps allow you to be a live broadcasting company.

A good approach to using Facebook Live is to hop on it and talk about your new blog post. Share some aspect of the content that you may not have shared in the post, such as your story and motivation behind why you wrote the post. Let viewers know they can click the link to your website to read the entire post.

STEP #5: PINTEREST

Not many lawyers are using Pinterest, and that's precisely why I recommend you jump on this platform! Upload the picture or screenshot relating to your blog post and add it to one or more of your Pinterest Boards. Several boards you may want to set up include current news, verdicts and settlements, legal tips, testimonials, videos, photos, podcasts, newsletters, and community service, just to name a few.

After using the content in your Word document to complete the description in Pinterest, make sure to add three to four relevant hashtags at the end, and also include your blog post link in the source link box. This way, when someone clicks on the picture, they will be taken to your blog post or website.

STEP #6: YOUTUBE

Video is huge on social media. Within a year of posting our first video (it wasn't very good, but it was a start), we received hundreds of new client inquiries and dozens of new cases. I was also featured in various high-profile websites, blogs, and the ABA Journal. Talk about good publicity!

If you haven't already done so, setup your YouTube channel and start making and posting short one- to three-minute-long videos. Also, share other interesting videos about your activities and events on your channel. People will relate to you when they learn more about your interests, passions, and family.

You don't need a fancy camera to create YouTube videos, and the process is simple. There are plenty of "how to" resources out there, but I think you'll figure things out once you complete and upload your first couple of videos. Using a lapel mic or earbuds will help make sure your audio is good (an important element to videos that many overlook).

By far, the best videos we've shared are the ones that do not look like they are professionally shot. For example, one involved me riding my mountain bike and using my smartphone to shoot a selfie video about why staying healthy will help you perform better and be a more effective trial lawyer. It received a great deal of favorable traction and feedback once I shared it on all the platforms.

Putting the camera up on a tripod at the office and sharing my take on a breaking news event (an approach called "newsjacking") has also resulted in articles on major blogs, national interviews, speaking engagements, and even being mentioned or profiled in more than one book. One bit of advice is to remember to pay attention to your background and how you look, and keep your video short and sweet.

Extra Tip: Here's a secret most people overlook. There are many services and programs that will allow you to get the audio of your video transcribed so that you can use it for a future blog post. Others will allow you to rip the audio from the video which you can then use as a podcast (more fully described below). Rip the audio and use it as a separate podcast!

The key is to keep things interesting and snappy. Don't be a boring lawyer. Don't sit behind your desk and sound like blah, blah, blah. When I look back, I'm embarrassed to watch my first dozen videos. But guess what - it was a learning process, and in the long run, it's all good.

STEP #7: SLIDESHARE
This often-overlooked platform is well respected and used successfully by marketing pros around the globe. I neglected this platform for far too long.

Once I decided to get active on SlideShare, I uploaded a "how to" presentation about negotiation, and within the first 24 hours it had more than 900 views and trended on Twitter and SlideShare. The response was so good that this presentation was then profiled on the SlideShare home page. Two days later, we were over 2,000 views. To date, we're up to 39,000+ views. You can and should do the same thing. Share your secret sauce.

Everything you do as a lawyer is based on steps and checklists. Take the material you already have that can help consumers (e.g., "10 Things to Know and Do If You're Arrested" or "6 Steps to a Successful Patent"), create compelling and easy to read PowerPoint slides, and then upload them to SlideShare. Take the blog post we've been talking about and break it down to a fifteen- to twenty-slide presentation. Link back to your original blog post.

STEP #8: PODCASTS

Podcasts are very popular because mobile technology now allows us to easily listen to podcasts anytime and anyplace. Take your blog post and turn the content into a short ten to twenty-minute podcast. Start with a snappy and attention-grabbing intro and then share your information using your own voice. Use your post as an outline and just share your message from your heart. Close with a call to action referring to your website or blog.

Podcast interviews are also a great way to expand your sphere of influence. Once you're up and running, reach out and interview other people who your listeners might find interesting. When done, share the link with the guest you interviewed, and he or she will almost always share the podcast with their audience. This is a great way to expand your sphere of influence and increase the number of eyeballs to your website's, blog's, and podcast's platforms.

There are plenty of resources out there to help get you started but a good place to start is the "how to" podcast sites by experts Pat Flynn or Cliff Ravenscraft.

Once we add and upload a podcast to our host (we use Libsyn), we share the podcast link back at our original post. We also upload and link to Stitcher, iTunes, and Soundcloud.

Note, once my podcasts are completed and uploaded, I share the unique links of these three platforms to most of the aforementioned social platforms. The heading and short description are changed from the earlier descriptions and posts. Links are also shared on the original blog post or website page, just in case a visitor would rather listen to the material instead of reading the blog post. My new podcast is at MitchJacksonPodcast.com.

STEP #9: BLUEJEANS, BELIVE.TV AND SIMILAR VIDEO SERVICES

These live video platforms allow you to have your own internet television show. For me, services like BlueJeans have been awesome platforms that have connected me with interesting and well-known people from all around the world. Using these types of services, I've been on shows with Katie Couric, Anderson Cooper, and one episode even ended up on TMZ. How cool is that?!

Some of the people I've interviewed are New York Times best-selling authors and celebrities with 250,000 to 1,000,000 Twitter followers. What do you think happens when they tweet out that they're going to be on my show?

You can use these platforms to interview guests about legal topics or approaches. I'd also recommend that you do what I do and, depending on your passion, reach out and interview people associated with your unique interests. Your show may not have anything to do with the law, but it will highlight the real you to your audience. This allows people to become interested in you as a human being, and that's a good thing!

Promote your show on all the platforms before and after the event (they're recorded). Share the show links and embed the video of your interview on your blog and platforms. Depending on the platform and guests, some of my shows have had more than 1,000 unique views within the first hour or so and several thousand in the first 24 hours. Lifelong friends have been made directly from using these platforms.

As I mentioned in the YouTube section, you may also want to have your interviews transcribed or audio ripped for future use on blogs and podcasts. Rarely is there a need to duplicate your efforts!

My live video show is TheShow.live. It's one of the longest, if not the longest running weekly live video show on the internet. My guests are people from around the world who are disrupting industries and creating global change.

What does that have to do with law? Nothing. What does this have to do with creating new global relationships with people who know, like, and trust you (and refer to you)? Everything!

STEP #10: INSTAGRAM AND SNAPCHAT

Whether you "get it" or not, millennials are using these platforms more than almost any other generation. As such, they're becoming more and more relevant in the business world. Several high-profile marketing experts are very keen on the future of these platforms.

This in and of itself is a good reason to get involved in these channels. Set up accounts and start using these platforms to share legal tips in a fun way.

Take the screenshot image of the blog post and share it on Instagram with a link or reference back to your website or blog. Share a tweet letting everyone know you've just posted a new Snapchat or Instagram.

Instagram Live

Instagram just rolled out new live streaming video options known as Instagram Live. I encourage you to embrace these new live video options and share your personal insight on a social media post you shared earlier that day. Give a behind-the-scenes look at something unique about why, where or how you created your post. Let your live viewers know they can read and share the post by going to a specific link.

STEP #11: PERISCOPE

Just like Facebook Live, Periscope allows you to live stream from your smartphone or tablet to the world. It's owned by Twitter, and your live video will appear in your Twitter feed.

When I have new content to share, I like to jump on Periscope from wherever I am and share the news with my audience. I usually share a backstory too as to why I wrote the post, and I always make sure to let my viewers know where they can find the full post.

I've also found Periscope to be a fun and powerful engagement tool at community events, as well as while flying my drone over the Pacific (yes, I live stream on both Periscope and Facebook Live while flying and engage in real-time conversation). The only limit to using Periscope is your imagination, so always be ready to pull your smartphone or tablet out and "go live" on Periscope.

STEP #12: MEDIUM

This blogging platform is a great tool to reach an entirely different audience than who may be following your law firm blog. I repurpose important or popular posts on Medium and am amazed at the additional traction I get when I do so. Often, I'll spend quality time rewriting the post before sharing on Medium. As with everything else, include pictures and embed videos when you can.

STEP #13: GOOGLE PLUS

Although Google Plus isn't a big priority for Google anymore, I still believe it's an important part of repurposing content. Whenever I re-purpose on Google Plus, I always see the content get indexed and displayed by the Google search engine. That is the reason, in and of itself, to take a minute or two to share on this platform.

Google Plus also allows for communities and my "Trial Lawyer Tips" Community now has over 4,000 members.

FINAL THOUGHTS

The above approach of repurposing content works very well. You don't have to overcomplicate the process for repurposing your work.

A single blog post can be shared using the above method over several days, weeks, and even months. Whatever works for you is fine. Just make sure to consistently take action.

Keep in mind that what's important on social media is the 80% part of the equation – that is, engaging and helping others. However, when I do jump over to the 20% side of things, this is exactly how I get things done.

Without a doubt, the best increase in influence and engagement I've experienced on the digital platforms have come from my efforts relating to other interests that complement the practice of law. When I blog about a legal theory or explain new statutes or case law, all I usually hear are digital crickets. But when I share a blog or social media post about my passions, family, youth sports, or family trips, the interaction and feedback is very strong.

It's with that interaction where the relationships are formed. And just like in the offline world, good relationships result in new referrals and business.

For example, I have a live streaming and social media blog at www. Streaming.Lawyer (no, that's not a typo, it doesn't end in .com). This is where I enjoy sharing daily live streaming and social media, business, entrepreneur, and legal tips. This blog is my passion, and I enjoy providing useful ideas to consumers to help with their businesses and online efforts. When I post here and then repurpose the content like I described above, I usually get great traction and engagement. This often leads to new speaking opportunities, interviews, and clients. You can do the same thing.

Using this approach and over time, trust and rapport are established with people (my "tribe") who share a common interest. When my global tribe has a legal question, or someone needs a lawyer, who do you think they reach out to?

CONCLUSION

Today, smart lawyers use social media to inspire, inform, educate, and build new relationships. Hopefully, you will use some, or maybe even all, of these repurposing ideas to do the same thing. I encourage you to use the different approaches in this chapter and start incorporating social media into your daily activity to expand your sphere of influence and create top-of-mind awareness.

But remember one thing: Creating content and engaging on social media the right way take time. Be patient and consistent in your efforts. Don't be afraid to be real and transparent. Don't be afraid to show your human side. I believe good things will happen if you do!

CHAPTER 13

FIVE POWER TIPS FOR DOMINATING FACEBOOK LEGAL MARKETING

By David Bitton

As an author, CLE speaker, and founder of PracticePanther.com, David is dedictaed to automating law firms with the help of today's technology. He's revolutionizing the legal industry by helping lawyers get more done in less time using PracticePanther's practice management software.

CHAPTER 13

Five Power Tips for Dominating Facebook Legal Marketing

By David Bitton

WHY FACEBOOK?

Facebook is almost a "no-brainer." It's free, personalized, targeted, and if your target market is consumers rather than businesses, Facebook is an awesome tool. Your business will have the opportunity to identify itself to your audience in any way you wish! Most of your law firm's branding and marketing can usually be attributed to the content posted on your Facebook fan page for your law firm. After figuring out what your key audience would be interested in viewing, there are endless posts you can create. Using humor while still being informational is a great approach to creating and keeping an audience.

But what do I write about?

1. Stories of how you helped your clients.
2. Stories of what happens if you DON'T hire a legal professional.
3. Client testimonials (pictures of letters, screenshots of emails, video testimonials).
4. Legal tips of the week.
5. Pictures of your office or the attorneys and paralegals with background stories.

POWER TIP #1 – HAVE A CONTEST!

The first marketing strategy that can help attract new customers through friends of friends is having a contest! Simply create a Facebook contest and offer something valuable in return (maybe a free consultation, 20% off, etc.). It not only helps get your current and prospective customers involved, it also increases page activity with the stream of new comments and likes you should be receiving if done properly.

POWER TIP #2 – FACEBOOK TARGETED ADS

Facebook is wildly successful and gaining traction in the online marketing industry because of its ability to target advertisements to immaculate laser-pointed accuracy. Consider how much they know about you and your customers and how far their reach is. You can target ads to men, women, people in relationships, married couples, anyone with specific keywords or affiliations, age, location, and MUCH more. Their prices are rather reasonable as you can pay per click or per impression (how many people see your ad). Many people recommend trying this method and spending a few hundred dollars to see how many clicks and conversions it brings to your firm. If it's working, keep it going. If not, move on to a different strategy.

POWER TIP #3 – BOOSTING A POST (SPONSORED STORIES)

There are times that you realize a recent post has been wildly successful, garnering tons of clicks, shares, and comments. Facebook will even let you know, "This post is doing better than 90% of your recent posts." This is the type of post you want to boost to get even more attention, as you seemed to have gotten lucky with a successful post and you want to capitalize on that. Boosting a post is fairly simple. Click on "Boost" on the bottom right when creating it, or click on the arrow at the top of the post and select "Boost." What this does is allow you to pay $5 and get hundreds of more people to see your posts. In recent years, Facebook has greatly limited the amount of people who see each of your posts. Only about 2-3% of your fans will actually see your posts these days. By boosting, you can increase your reach to more of your fans and their friends, as well.

POWER TIP #4 – USING FACEBOOK ADS MANAGER

After you boost a post, go to your Facebook Ads manager (on the top right) and try removing the ad targeting friends of friends, since you only care only about YOUR customers at this point to get the most exposure for your money. A $5 boost will go a long way to reaching all of your customers, as Facebook only shows your post to 2% of your fans if you don't boost it. You could also do this now when boosting a post, but you will still have a lot more flexibility and advanced options if you get familiar with this tool. This is a more advanced option, so feel free to ignore it, or do a bit more research on Google before diving into it.

POWER TIP #5 – FACEBOOK OPEN GRAPH

Facebook launched its Open Graph API in recent years, and with it came plug-ins that you can easily drop into your website – for instance, the like button, activity feed, friends who like your page, and more. This allows you to make your website more social and show that you're part of the modern social world. I would recommend using most of these on your website's blog (you do have a blog, right?). Usually, you will find all the plugins and widgets on the right sidebar of the blog as well as Facebook like or share links embedded at the top or bottom of each blog post. If you're not sure how to do this, hop onto UpWork.com and search for a Facebook and WordPress expert, and they can do it for you for probably under $20. Tell them you want to install a Facebook widget to the right sidebar of your blog that shows the number of fans you have and a button to like the page right from your blog. Disclaimer - if you're going to show off your Facebook page on your website or blog, you better make sure you have at least more than 200 fans, or you will look like a very small law firm.

BONUS POWER TIP #6 – USING HOOTSUITE.COM TO AUTOMATE FACEBOOK CONTENT

I know, I know - I said five power tips, but I had to throw this sixth one in as a bonus. And, I know we've mentioned it before, but it's worth mentioning again. Creating numerous posts every day or week seems tedious, time consuming, and often exhausting. And it sure can be. But when you get in the zone and start creating posts, your creativity is unleashed, and you can hopefully churn out tons of good content within an hour. Using a website like HootSuite.com allows you to schedule posts on Facebook, Twitter, LinkedIn, Google Plus, and more, all in one shot. Give their free version a try; it currently lets you post on three social networks for free. You should also look into Buffer.com and MeetEdgar.com as great alternatives or complimentary products.

BONUS POWER TIP #7 – THE BEST BOOKS TO PURCHASE

I know what you're thinking, and yes, I'm on a roll with these power tips! If you're serious about Facebook marketing, I highly suggest going to Amazon and buying a book called *Ultimate Guide to Facebook Advertising* by Perry Marshall. As of this writing, his book on Facebook is the #1 best- seller in the Social Media for Business category on Amazon. In fact, I am personally obsessed with all of his books. I actually read his Ultimate Guide to Google AdWords in one night, and it's over 400 pages long. And his book *80/20 Sales and Marketing* is one of the best books I've ever read. Go get them – you won't be disappointed.

If you're going to spend any money online, or even outsource to an expert, I still recommend reading these books so you can have a knowledgeable conversation and not be taken advantage of. You know your business better than anyone else, and you will get tons of ideas you can implement or delegate after reading these books.

Hopefully you'll be on your way to a profitable Facebook ad campaign in the next few weeks. Good luck!

CHAPTER 14

SECRETS OF LEGAL MARKETING - WHAT YOU SHOULD BE DOING NOW

By Andrew Cabasso

—

Andrew Cabasso is a practicing attorney and VP of Web Services at Uptime Legal where he runs JurisPage, an Internet Marketing firm specializing in online presence solutions for law firms including website design, SEO, and search marketing. He has given many lectures and CLEs on website design and Internet marketing to legal professionals.

CHAPTER 14

Secrets of Legal Marketing – What You Should Be Doing Now

By Andrew Cabasso

If your law firm has ever tinkered with online marketing, whether it's search optimization, advertising, social media, or email marketing, you may have decided: "This can't work for my practice." Sometimes that's the right call. Sometimes it doesn't work. Other times, that conclusion is based on bad data.

Not every law firm that runs an advertising campaign is doing it right, even if the Google reps set up your campaign. Not every email marketing campaign is going to produce results, especially if you don't know what you're doing. And, not every blogging / SEO campaign will produce results if you don't have the right strategy.

So, now we're going to dispel some myths and show you – from people who have found the online marketing success you're looking for – what you need to create effective online marketing campaigns. Let's start with advertising.

ONLINE ADVERTISING

Advertising is one of those areas where you can waste a ton of money if you don't know what you're doing – in particular, Google AdWords. And for a lot of lawyers who are just getting started, there are a lot of common mistakes.

First, recognize that when Google's team calls you up to "help" build an advertising campaign, they want you to spend as much money as possible. They aren't going to be limiting keywords or negative keywords.

Take Google's advice with a grain of salt. Even with a well-optimized campaign, you might find that it costs a lot to get clicks, calls, and clients. So what can you do?

THE BEST PRACTICE AREAS FOR ADVERTISING

Not every practice area can "kill it" in online advertising. In our experience, the best-performing ad campaigns are those that are more consumer-oriented practice areas.

Practice areas that tend to do well with advertising, in our experience, are:

- Family law
- Personal injury
- Criminal defense / DUI
- Estate planning
- Employee-side employment law
- Immigration
- Patent law
- Residential real estate

That's not to say that you can't have a business law or commercial real estate practice and get some traffic or business via an advertising campaign. However, there tends to be less search volume for those areas, comparatively.

SPEAKING MY LANGUAGE

One secret to share is that there is a much less competitive way to advertise online. I'm talking about non-English-language campaigns. AdWords in Spanish for practice areas like auto accident lawyer is much less expensive than its English-language counterpart.

The catch is, you have to have the person answering your phone be fluent in the language for which you are advertising. Whether you have a paralegal, secretary, or answering service, they have to be able to communicate with your callers.

PLATFORMS

Google AdWords gets a ton of traffic, which is usually why it's the go-to for law firms advertising online, but it's not the only option out there.

Here are a few other great alternatives:

Bing Ads – With Bing, you can instantly copy over an existing Google AdWords campaign and reach an expanded audience. All you have to do is click the prominent "Import Campaign" button, connect your AdWords account, and Bing does the work for you. The beauty of Bing is that it can be relatively little additional work if you are already advertising on Google, and you get more clicks - often for a deep discount. Because Bing's search engine gets much less traffic than Google, it's not as competitive for advertisers. However, you could still do well to get more clicks, calls, and clients by dominating the space.

Facebook Ads – Other authors already mentioned this, but it's worth mentioning again: Facebook has a lot of specific data on its users. It's scary. But with that data, you can target a very specific profile of the type of person to whom you want to advertise. Reaching people on Facebook is less expensive than advertising on AdWords, so for many firms, it's an appealing option if you don't have a large enough budget to be able to get results in AdWords.

AdRoll – AdRoll is a retargeting service, meaning you can show ads to people who have already visited your website. The cost per view (AdRoll doesn't have a cost-per-click model like AdWords does) is relatively low. A retargeting strategy can help you ensure that if someone visited your website and didn't reach out to you, they would see your ads all over the internet, enticing them to come back.

SEARCH ENGINE OPTIMIZATION

Targeting your local geographic area is king now when it comes to search engine optimization. Google's algorithm promotes local-oriented search results. Of course, when people search for a lawyer, they generally want to see those in their local area.

For law firms, this means optimizing your search presence to show up more visibly on Google Maps. When people search for "local divorce lawyer," or whatever your practice area is, Google Maps will show the results based on the area they're searching from.

To get better visibility in Google Maps, getting directory listings is important. Get profiles for your law firm in every local online directory you can, from Yellow Pages.com to Manta, Super Pages, Avvo, Yelp, and more. The single most important one? Google My Business, formerly known as Google Places.

Create and verify your Google My Business profile before you do anything else. That should be Step 1. Then, go out and create as many directory profiles as you can. Simply go to Google and type in, "Google My Business" to get started and create your Google business profile.

One important caveat: Make sure that your name, address, and phone number are 100% consistent.

If your office address is "123 Main Street, Suite 456," make sure that every listing has it typed the same way. You shouldn't then also use "Ste. 456" or "#456." Pick one and stick to it.

Once you have your Google Business profile set up, ask your happy clients to give you positive reviews. The best recommendation is to screen clients after an engagement ends. Ask them how satisfied they were with your representation and to fill out a brief survey. If their responses are positive, give them a link to your Google business page to leave a review.

BLOGGING AND CONTENT CREATION

A big mistake we see a lot with search optimization is law firms blogging too infrequently, or not blogging about the right things. Blogging about some esoteric areas of law when your target audience is lay people who don't care about the Supreme Court is not the way to go.

Here are a few recommendations for blog topic ideation.

The first step in creating content for your blog is simple: research what your competitors are doing. See which topics are covered often and add them to your list. Identify their FAQ posts and other popular posts, and then write better blogs than them.

Consider what fresh perspective you can add that other attorneys may have overlooked. Rework the topic from another angle and answer in a way that best reflects your audience. FAQ posts are great because the questions your clients ask you in intake interviews are also being searched for online. Consider some alternatives to blogging that may allow your content to reach a broader audience. For example, you might invest in a well-designed, educational infographic.

Think about how far this piece of content could go. Upon uploading it to your own site, these would do well on social media and would be great to offer to relevant blogs, even a local community website.

Instead of just focusing on answering client questions, create a Google Alert on your phone for issues related to your industry. For example, if you're a family law attorney, set up alerts for topics such as child education, child nutrition, and co-parenting solutions and see how much traffic you'll drive from your target audience. Go to Google.com/alerts to create your first alert.

The key here is that you're attracting leads at various stages, so while they might not have a need for your services now, you'll be the first they think of when they do. Moreover, your quality content will signal to Google that your site is relevant, and you'll see your rank and domain authority increase over time.

SOCIAL MEDIA

(For this part, let's keep "social media advertising" out of the equation and just focus on the unpaid aspect of social media).

Social media can be dangerous. With the latest algorithm updates, chances are that your firm's recent posts probably won't be seen by your audience. It can be a big time-suck for little return. And return can be hard to measure. After all, how many tweets, Facebook posts, comments, or likes does it take to get a new client?

So why bother? What's the strategy with social media? The strategy I recommend is to focus on it as a referral-building endeavor. Don't publish content necessarily to get your readers to become clients. Get them to refer clients to you.

Most of the people following your firm are probably not your ideal client anyway. They are probably friends, family, and colleagues - the exact type of people who can and will refer you business. Plus, you've probably seen the types of posts that scream "Buy my service." It comes across desperate, and there's little reason for other people to engage with that content.

So, share your latest successes. Share your wins. Share your recent news. Share your blog posts. But come at this from a perspective of "I want to stay top-of-mind in the audience's brains so that when they have a case to refer in my practice area, they immediately think of me."

With that strategy in mind for posting, commenting, and engaging with others, you'll reduce the likelihood of wasted effort.

EMAIL MARKETING

Email marketing is like social media, as it can be very effective in keeping you top-of-mind with potential referral sources.

Email is great because it:
- is inexpensive
- is likely to be received and read
- has a high return on investment

If you have a growing email list, sharing newsletters with your recent news, analysis of practice area developments, and achievements, it reminds people that you are a skilled lawyer and that if they should ever encounter someone who needs your services, they would be in good hands with you.

Email tends to be more effective than social media because emails get delivered 99% of the time – so your recipient will most likely at the very least see your email in their inbox.

With social media, there's only a 2% chance that any given audience member sees your post. Pound-for-pound, email marketing is king. In addition to regular newsletters, "drip campaigns" can also help you get some wins. Drip campaigns are a burst of several sequential emails related to a topic. Typically, you get drip emails when you sign up for a new online service.

You probably know the cadence:
- Email 1: You have signed up, congratulations.
- Email 2: Thank you for signing up; let us know if you have any questions.
- Email 3: Here are some cool features of our software.
- Email 4: Here are more cool features of our software.
- Email 5: Here's a small case study of someone who loves our software.

- Email 6: Your free trial is ending; pay us for our software to keep using it.
- Email 7: Seriously, your free trial is over. Pay us or lose access.

Law firms can actually get new business with the help of a drip campaign in combination with a downloadable offer. For law firms, drip campaigns can work well if you have a downloadable e-book or guide on your website that people can download. If someone downloads your e-book on "Child Custody Issues in Divorce," chances are they probably need a lawyer. So, they could probably use some more education.

After the potential client clicks the download button, they should, over the next few days to a few weeks, get several emails that help educate them and get them to reach out to your firm for a consultation.

The cadence can look like this:
- Email 1: Your email address is confirmed; download your e-book here.
- Email 2: Let us know if you have any questions about the e-book.
- Email 3: Let me educate you a little more about the topic.
- Email 4: Let me educate you even more about this topic, still for free.
- Email 5: Let me tell you about our firm, and our work that's related to the e-book topic.
- Email 6: Do you need help / want to schedule a consultation?

Something like that. You get the idea.

MARKETING MANAGEMENT

This area needs the most talking about. You can spend thousands of dollars on building and running marketing campaigns, but if you are not managing them well, you will waste a lot of money.

In our experience helping law firms with their marketing, we've helped firms that were generating new potential clients but were unable to get them to sign a retainer.

Often the biggest issues are in the firm's management of its leads and intake process.

Really, there are a few things that need to be addressed separately:
- Processes
- Call Tracking
- Intake
- CRM
- Follow-Up
- Engagement

PROCESSES

The first step is to take a look at the big picture of your new client workflow. You should know the answer to these questions:
- Who answers your phone when someone calls your firm?
- What happens when someone calls off-hours?
- How quickly before a lawyer responds?
- How are they tracked through your pipeline?
- How long before they get a consultation?
- How often do you follow up after the consultation to get a signed retainer?
- How long before they retain?
- How do you get and process the retainer?

If you don't know the answer, or your answer is "It depends – sometimes this happens or sometimes that happens," there needs to be a standardization to that aspect of your process. You can't treat new client leads from the internet the same way you've historically treated referrals.

Referrals will probably come back to you if you don't get back to them right away. Internet visitors will not.

Someone who visits your website and calls your firm has nothing keeping them tied to your firm. You have to pick up the phone when they call the first time, or you're going to be much more likely to lose them as a potential client. If someone is referred to your firm, they want to work with you. You and your services were recommended to them, and they most likely will give you a chance.

But if someone is in urgent need of a lawyer and turns to the internet, they'll do some research, call the first lawyer they qualify, and if that is you and you don't get back to them right away, they may call the second or third or fourth. If one of those is reached, they may never come back to you.

This is why standardized processes for your intake and retention are critically important. You can optimize your marketing so well that you generate new potential clients. But if you can't handle them properly, you're throwing money away, resulting in a much higher cost to get a new client.

With that being said, here are some recommendations and tools to help you optimize your pipeline for new client calls and retention.

CALL TRACKING

You need to know where your potential clients are coming from. Whether it's getting your number from a business card or clicking an ad or social media post or email or organic search traffic, you have to be able to account for everything. Otherwise, how do you know if your campaigns are working?

You can spend $5,000 per month on an ad campaign, but if all you know is, "They said they found me through Google," you don't know if that means organic or paid. You could be running a terrible paid ad campaign and not know it.

The way to remedy that is to sign up for a call tracking service. In particular, we recommend CallRail. Call tracking essentially assigns a phone number or a pool of multiple phone numbers for your firm to use. You get phone numbers on your website, in your print advertisements, or on your business card, and when a prospective client calls the number, they reach your firm's main phone number.

Meanwhile, each call gets logged in your call tracking system as one new lead. It also takes down your visitor's caller ID, the call duration, their location (if available), and what page they visited on your website when they called.

Some lawyers are concerned about the idea of having a phone number that isn't the firm's main office phone number on their business card, TV ad, or website. But the benefits outweigh the costs. Here, you actually get to know how people found you and attribute every single lead to the appropriate marketing channel.

I use call tracking numbers on my business cards; this way, I know when someone came to me via a referral. Believe it or not, lawyers have been doing this for years. At the end of the day, the callers are routed to any phone number you choose – office, cell phone, whatever – and you get access to an amazing amount of data that breaks down for you how many calls you're getting each month based on your referral sources.

Imagine if you knew for certain that your Yellow Pages ad got you exactly two phone calls. While you may have had a hunch, call tracking proves it.

INTAKE

What happens when someone calls your firm? Do you have an answering service or a receptionist? What happens when it's after-hours? Are you running a paid ad campaign when you are not able to answer the phone? If so, that's potentially a huge waste of advertising spend.

Run a test. Call into your law firm and go through the process yourself (or have a friend do it and give you feedback). Do you receive a friendly greeting? We've seen that some firms have had customer experience issues because of rude, impatient, or inattentive staff who answer the phone.

This is the first direct encounter someone has with your firm, so don't overlook it. Make sure that whoever answers the phone is friendly, polite, and gets all the information they need to pass off to a lawyer. Everything must go into your CRM software, and the next steps are ready to go.

CRM

How are your potential clients being tracked by the firm? Leads should not just be handed off to a lawyer. Often, you will need to call your potential clients back multiple times, leaving several voicemails and sending a few emails before hearing back from them.

If you are not tracking what has been done for a potential client and what you have to do next, you potentially lose them.

FOLLOW-UP

Some firms get a new lead and reach out only once. If you end up leaving a voicemail or even reaching them the first time, you still need to follow up until the retainer agreement is signed. Keep reaching out, every day or every other day, until the potential client either tells you "Please call me back on X day," "Let's get started," or "I hired another lawyer." Without a definitive response from the potential client, assume they are still figuring things out, and follow-up with them politely, but often.

A big mistake I've seen many firms make is having a 30-minute free consultation, and then not following up. The firm assumes: "If they're interested they will call back." And that's not always the case. Sometimes they get distracted or busy. You should continually follow-up until you get a "yes" or a "no."

ENGAGEMENT

When you get that "yes," the easier and quicker it is to get that client across the finish line, the better. Make signing a retainer agreement as effortless as possible. Use e-signature software like DocuSign or HelloSign.

WRAPPING THINGS UP

You don't need to make all the common mistakes that many firms make with their marketing. Plenty of law firms have found success with building their business by implementing these strategies. Take a page out of their book. Save yourself time and expense by building your marketing campaigns right, from the ground up. I know these tips will help you get ahead of the curve.

Best of luck!

MULTI-PLATFORM PUBLISHING & SCHEDULIING

By Nick Rishwain

Nick Rishwain, JD, is Vice President of Client Relations & Development for Experts.com, an online marketing platform for expert witnesses and consultants. In his free time, he is quite active in social media. He founded and co-hosts a live video podcast, LegalTechLIVE, which evangelizes the advancements in the legal technology sector.

CHAPTER 15

Multi-Platform Publishing & Scheduling

By Nick Rishwain

In March of 2017, PracticePanther's Saul Landesman reached out to me about doing a webinar regarding digital marketing for attorneys. Having done webinars and live videos about this topic before, I wondered how I could make this webinar different. So many webinars are about the exact same things: content marketing, social media marketing, Facebook ads, etc.

At the risk of sounding cliché, I tried to find something that might be "actionable" for law firm implementation. Saul and I seemed to have a meeting of the minds on not over-complicating digital/social marketing. In my experience, most lawyers need to begin using social media platforms. The others who are using the platforms need to learn how to do so consistently. Consistently publishing requires some tools to do so efficiently. I'll get into the tools shortly, but first, I'm going to lay out the five major platforms a law firm needs to consider (not every platform available).

There are five social media power houses where attorneys could be spending their time and energy. I intentionally did not say you "should" be spending your time and energy on these platforms. You don't have to spend time on all of these. Just be aware that these are probably the most valuable to those in the legal industry and law-related services.

- Facebook (Facebook Live)
- LinkedIn
- Twitter (Periscope/Twitter Live)
- Instagram (Instagram Live)
- YouTube (YouTube Live)

Many authors in this book have covered a few of these tools, but I will be diving into the live aspects of them and going a little deeper. We will also discuss some cross-platform publishing and repurposing of your content.

PUBLISHING TOOLS:

There are two primary social media scheduling tools used for small-to-medium sized businesses. Buffer and Hootsuite. I, like many other authors in this book, use Buffer personally and professionally. However, I have friends who are very pleased with HootSuite. Other tools exist for large enterprise operations and may be more appropriate for larger law firms.

Buffer and Hootsuite are content publishing platforms. They allow you to schedule and publish content to your social networks. As my experience is with Buffer, we'll use it for the remainder of this section.

My professional use of Buffer is generally targeted to the platforms of Facebook (Profiles, pages, groups), Twitter, LinkedIn, and Google+. Cautionary note to lawyers: Your clients are not on Google+. However, if a scheduling tool gives you access to post there, you might as well post there. Do not expect Google+ to give you a great deal of traction or visibility. Others in this book have pointed out the SEO benefits to posting to Google+, but we are not discussing SEO in this chapter.

TYPES OF CONTENT:

Now that you have ideas for some tools that will make it easy for you to publish across multiple channels, let's talk about what kind of content you should post:

- Blog Posts
- Images & Photos
- Video
- Live Video
- Webinars

There are dozens of other ideas for content, but let's keep it focused and stick to the items above. First off, do what is most comfortable. Think of the items above as interchangeable. You don't have to come up with a new topic every time you want to post something. Many pieces of content are going to be reused (repurposed).

BLOG POSTS:

I conducted a poll during a live webinar with PracticePanther and many of their members. We confirmed what experience had already suggested: about two-thirds of law firms are sharing their blog posts on social media more than any other piece of content.

Here are some suggested topics for your blog: frequently asked questions, discussion of charitable or community participation, case studies, anecdotes, interesting cases (even if it wasn't one of your own), etc.

IMAGES & PHOTOS:

You have a smart phone; start using it smartly! In fact, you probably have a bunch of photos in your camera roll that can be used to post to your social channels. In today's crowded marketplace, you have to give your brand a personality. You are your brand. You have to be the personality. As such, you're going to have to share photos of yourself.

Images are a little different. Buffer has a free image creation tool called Pablo. This will allow you to use stock images and overlay text in the event you don't have a photo to share. You may occasionally want to share a short post communicating a quick message. Use Pablo or Canva to create images with ease.

Here are some ideas of photos to share: you in the community, with your family, at your hobby, at the office, with your pets, in front of the courthouse, taking the office out for lunch, and anything else that shows you being a real person, and even having some fun. Just by taking a quick look at PracticePanther's Instagram page, we can see that photos of their office dog Nala garner more comments, likes, and shares than almost any other post. Show off your personality; people want to see the behind the scenes!

As for images, you may wish to create things such as posts with small pieces of positive advice or encouragement, an image with a link to a free resource, a gavel image with a short message, an image that represents what you do, a "Happy Friday" image. The more you do it, the more creative you'll become.

VIDEO:

If you are not already using video to market your law firm, I strongly recommend getting comfortable with the idea of doing so. According to a 2016 survey by Hubspot.com, "social video generates 1,200% more shares than text and images combined." The same survey found, "Video on a landing page can increase conversations by 80% or more." These are important numbers, as the effectiveness of video marketing is only growing.

When it comes to making a video, you do not want to cover the standard legal issues (i.e., what to do after a car accident, DUI, why you should have an estate plan, etc.). You should try to be a little more creative in developing informational videos.

Some ideas for videos are similar to those for photos above: you doing something fun or exciting like enjoying your hobby, an interview of a local leader, an update on new legislation, commentary on Supreme Court decisions (if it affects your clients), or answering frequently asked questions. Notice, I put the fun, exciting, and hobby-centered ideas at the forefront of potential topics. Those topics allow the viewer to really get to know you as a person, rather than you as a lawyer. This is an endearing tactic intended for the viewer to begin to know, like, and trust you (forgive the overused phraseology).

LIVE VIDEO:

Live video (also known as a social video) can be used in much the same way as recorded video. People love live videos because they're more authentic, less polished, and they allow viewers to comment and have a conversation with you in real-time.

Four of the five platforms mentioned have live video components. The social media platforms are putting serious emphasis on live video production and interaction.

One way you may wish to use live video is to create a weekly live video show, interview local guests, and answer new or frequently asked questions.

If you are going to have a guest, make the show about the guest, but do not forget to watch for comments from the live audience. Participation is key. I highly recommend that you not make your live show about your practice area or you won't have a live audience.

Right now, Facebook loves live video, and they're promoting it heavily in everyone's news feed. If you do a live video on Facebook, it will get significantly more exposure and views than a regular video you upload or share. You probably noticed a few times that Facebook will alert you if someone is doing a live video right now, causing even more views. The most important part about recording live video is preparation. You want to create a bullet-pointed list of what you're going to speak about and practice before recording. The worst thing that could happen is messing up in the middle and having to cancel, especially if people are watching. Not to worry - there typically aren't any viewers who watch your video live anyhow. The only time you can expect people to watch your videos live is if your fans knows you're going to record a live video at a certain time, or it's longer than 10 minutes and the right time of day when your friends and fans are on Facebook. Almost all of your views will be after the live video is finished, as Facebook will heavily promote that video much higher up in the news feed than other regular videos. After the live interview is complete, you can download it from Facebook and upload it to YouTube to share across Twitter, Google+, LinkedIn, your blog, email newsletter, and more.

REPURPOSING:

Once you have content that you can repurpose (blog posts, images, photos, videos, live videos, and webinars), you want to share that content on Facebook, Twitter, LinkedIn, Instagram, and YouTube. The scheduling tools are going to allow you to share across these platforms consistently.

BLOG POST EXAMPLE:

You will want to share a blog post across most platforms. You certainly cannot share a text blog post on YouTube, but you can reuse the topic to create a video at a later date. You will want to share your newly minted blog post on Facebook, LinkedIn, Twitter, Instagram, and probably on Google+.

VIDEO EXAMPLE:

Another lawyer friend, Daryl Dixon, has become quite proficient at creating videos. He does some short daily videos, recorded videos, and live videos. He creates short "DailyDaryl" videos which he uploads to YouTube and shares on Facebook and Twitter at different days and times. You may want to take a look just to get some ideas.

WEBINARS:

Webinars are the one area where you should speak about your practice and/or areas of expertise. Also, you may have a guest host come and speak about their area of expertise. You will have to do some pre-promotion of the webinar because you need an audience.

A webinar allows you to have a captive audience who is interested in the topic you are discussing (estate planning, trademark protection, IP infringement, etc.).

Make sure to record the webinar so you can reuse the content. When people ask what kind of a webinar to do, I recommend thinking about teaching a topic. If it is a webinar for attorneys, a more advanced topic would be applicable.

With webinars, you get the benefit of having live attendees in an exclusive setting. Further, you have already obtained the additional benefit of collecting email addresses so you can stay in touch with the attendees. Finally, if you have recorded the webinar, you can regularly re-share the information across multiple platforms.

PracticePanther is exceptionally good at creating and repurposing webinars. I recommend visiting their YouTube channel (www.youtube.com/practicepanther) to see how they host a webinar professionally.

You can use GoToWebinar for hosting webinars, or take a look at the more advanced WebinarJam if you want more options including the ability to pre-record webinars more easily. If you're going to invest in webinars, I recommend practicing beforehand, as many technical issues can come up in the middle.

And if you want to get really fancy, I know the PracticePanther folks use the Logitech C920 HD Webcam and Blue Snowball USB Microphone for high quality video and audio. You can get both on Amazon for under $100 total.

I hope you find this chapter helpful in your law firm promotional efforts. You can find me all over social media if you have any questions. Do not be afraid to reach out and connect.

LAW FIRM PRODUCTIVITY & AUTOMATION

THE ULTIMATE TOOLKIT FOR ATTORNEYS

By David Bitton

—

As an author, CLE speaker, and founder of PracticePanther.com, David is dedicated to automating law firms with the help of today's technology. He's revolutionizing the legal industry by helping lawyers get more done in less time using PracticePanther's practice management software.

CHAPTER 16

The Ultimate Toolkit for Attorneys

By David Bitton

Whether it is gaining visibility on the internet, scheduling social media posts, or managing your growing list of clients, we have compiled a list of some of the best productivity and marketing tools to streamline your workflow and make you more money. All prices shown below are at the time of publishing and most likely will change.

1. MICROSOFT OFFICE 365 ($8.25/USER/MONTH)

The classic staple of attorneys, Microsoft Office 365, offers a powerful suite of tools such as Word, PowerPoint, and Excel that help you draft and edit documents, generate spreadsheets, and create beautiful presentations. Although PowerPoint and Excel are useful tools, attorneys typically spend most of their time editing and drafting new documents and contracts in Word, making it the number-one essential tool for any attorney.

2. FILE STORAGE: DROPBOX OR BOX (FREE OR $5/USER/MONTH)

If you want to go paperless, moving your files to the cloud is one of the first steps you can take, besides investing in a scanner. With Box or Dropbox, you can relax knowing that all your files and documents are securely stored and backed up online without ever having to do a manual backup yourself. You can say goodbye to your expensive servers and finally be able to easily access your files from anywhere in the world on any device. You can even invite your colleagues or clients to collaborate with you and edit the documents together in real-time. You can restore deleted files or see any revisions made by you or someone else. And if you use a practice management software, you will most likely be able to integrate it with them, as well. With more attorneys focusing on efficiency and becoming less reliant on paper, Box and Dropbox can be critically essential tools for managing your legal documents.

3. TRACKING SOFTWARE: GOOGLE ANALYTICS (FREE)

Google Analytics is the most widely used free web analytics service on the internet. It allows you to track all the visitors coming to your site so you can see exactly where your online marketing efforts are paying off. You can see how visitors found your website, what page they landed on, what they searched for in Google to find you, how long they spent on your site, what city or state they're from, and much more. Google Analytics is the go-to resource for any attorney serious about tracking their online marketing efforts and return on investment on advertising. It also takes roughly 5 minutes to install, but we do recommend having an expert set it up for you correctly.

4. FREELANCE MARKETPLACE: UPWORK (HOURLY OR FLAT FEE)

Upwork.com is a global freelancing platform where businesses and independent professionals connect and collaborate remotely. The power of Upwork is in its platform, allowing you to hire freelancers in just about any part of the world in just a few clicks. Whether you're hiring a part-time paralegal or just need someone to write blog posts for your website, you can get your work done in less time and for a fraction of the price compared to hiring someone full-time.

5. VIDEO CONFERENCING: GO-TO-MEETING (STARTING AT $24/MONTH)

For attorneys who have out-of-town clients and want to save on travel expenses, Go-To-Meeting is a must-have tool. Go-To-Meeting is an online meeting, desktop sharing, and video conferencing software that enables you to meet with customers, clients, or colleagues via the internet in real time. You simply send your client a link, and you can share screens, speak by video chat, or even call into a conference number they give you.

6. PRINT MARKETING: VISTAPRINT (STARTING AT $10)

Vistaprint empowers millions of business owners worldwide to market themselves professionally. Whether you need your own business cards, signs and posters, corporate gifts, or any other marketing materials, VistaPrint can help you create the customized materials you need to get your message across. Because VistaPrint is catered to small businesses, you can order small quantities for affordable prices.

7. WEBSITE BUILDER: WORDPRESS (FREE OR PREMIUM)

A website, as everyone knows, is one of the most important branding and marketing strategies for your company. When someone thinks about you, hears about you, gets referred to you, or gets a business card from you, they will most likely look you up online. Fortunately, with a content management system like WordPress, you can select a template, and build your very own beautiful website. Simply insert a template, add text and images, click publish, and you're live! We strongly recommend WordPress, as it's the most customizable with by far the most templates and plugins online. If an attorney wants to make a good first impression with potential clients, having a professional website is the key to making this happen.

8. EMAIL MARKETING: MAILCHIMP (FREE OR PREMIUM)

MailChimp is a popular email marketing software for attorneys who want to send email newsletters and announcements to their clients online. The idea behind starting an email campaign is to start building an email list of leads, potential clients, or even current or past clients. Now you can start reminding them that you and your law firm exist via beautiful newsletters or monthly campaigns. When potential clients are looking for your services, you will always be at the top of their minds.

9. PAYMENT PROCESSING: LAWPAY

It is critical for attorneys to handle credit card transactions correctly, especially retainer payments to their trust accounts. In fact, according to LawPay, trust account violations are one of the most common reasons for disciplinary action. Fortunately, LawPay is designed to correctly separate earned and unearned fees to avoid commingling funds when accepting credit card payments. LawPay works with over 90 bar associations across the country, including the American Bar Association, to ensure their program is up-to-date and in compliance. You can even place a payment button on your website, so your clients can pay their invoices online, or make retainer payments directly into your trust account. The monthly fees range from only $5-$20, plus credit card processing fees. When signing up for a new LawPay account with PracticePanther, you can get your first six months of monthly fees completely waived. All you will pay for are the credit card transaction fees. If you accept credit card payments each month (after the first six months), your monthly fee will be waived as well. How's that for a deal?!

10. FUJITSU SCANSNAP IX500 SCANNER ($410)

If you truly want to go paperless, having a good scanner is the way to do it. All you need to do is purchase one and save all your scanned documents to Box.com or Dropbox. You never have to worry about losing another file while also being able to instantly find and share any file with your team or opposing counsel. The Fujitsu ScanSnap iX500 is the scanner of choice among law firms, as it can scan numerous documents at once and scans both the front and back. It will convert the document and PDF into editable and searchable text (very handy for conflict searches), a process called optical character recognition / OCR. That means it recognizes the characters on the paper and converts them to searchable text on your computer.

11. SCHEDULING SOFTWARE: ACUITYSCHEDULING (FREE OR PREMIUM)

Acuity Scheduling is an entirely web-based system for scheduling appointments and meetings with your clients. There is nothing to download, and it is completely responsive on any mobile device. The best part is sending your clients a link or embedding the calendar on your website, where they can schedule meetings whenever you're free. It links to your calendar so it knows when you're available.

12. BUSINESS PHONE: GOOGLE VOICE (FREE)

So you think you need a special office or business phone to carry around with you? Think again. With tools such as Google Voice, you can have your very own customized business phone number that will forward directly to your cell phone for free. The goal is to make and receive calls directly from your normal cell, but with a different phone number – without having to pay for another phone. You can also set up schedules so it can forward calls to different numbers at different times. For example, you can forward calls to your office during the day, and forward calls to your cell phone after-hours or weekends. If you miss a call, you also get a notification on your mobile app or via an email. And if someone leaves you a voicemail, it sends you an email and even transcribes it so you can just read what was said. Did we mention it's completely free?!

13. NOTE TAKING APP: EVERNOTE (FREE)

Evernote is a free app for your smartphone and computer that stores everything digital in your life in one app. Evernote works as one workspace that lives across your phone, tablet, and computer. You can collect information and find what you need in a simple search. Attorneys love using Evernote, because it enables them to keep track of ideas, store legal research, and share notebooks with business partners. Many of us simply use it for notes and personal to-do lists.

14. VIRTUAL RECEPTIONIST: RUBY RECEPTIONIST

Want your practice to look a lot bigger and more professional instantly? With a virtual receptionist. The most popular choice we recommend for a virtual secretary is Ruby Receptionists. With Ruby, you will make your clients think you have some big law office – without even having one! When someone calls your local or 800 number, a virtual secretary answers the phone professionally and exactly how you want them to using your exact script. They can help with filtering callers, blocking spammers and solicitors, and letting actual leads and clients through. You can also think of them as professional gatekeepers to keep you focused on your business. One of the most important things a client is looking for when hiring you is responsiveness. If you never answer the phone or return calls in a timely manner, they will go somewhere else. Almost everyone will agree that missed calls equal missed opportunities, making Ruby Receptionists an important tool for almost any attorney.

At the time of publishing, pricing starts at only $269/month for up to 100 receptionist minutes. Think of what you would pay a full-time receptionist per month, even if you find one for minimum wage! They say the average receptionist call time is 1 minute and 30 seconds, which equates to about 66 calls. By the way, Ruby was kind enough to provide the promo code PANTHERSOFTWARE to get $75 off your first invoice. Look how much money we're saving you already!

15. ELECTRONIC SIGNATURES: DOCUSIGN (STARTING AT $10/MONTH)

DocuSign has to be one of the most popular tools for attorneys to sign documents online. With DocuSign, you can quickly and securely access and sign documents, upload and send documents for others to sign, and send reminders any time. If you are an attorney who writes a lot of contracts and requires a lot of signing, DocuSign is the way to go.

16. PASSWORD MANAGER: LASTPASS (FREE OR PREMIUM)

Are you always having a hard time remembering your username and password? Do you use the same password for everything? Well, the hardship is over. LastPass is a useful tool that you can use to store all your log-in information and generate super secure 25 digit passwords for each website. You can even fill in any form with your contact information, which is extremely useful when purchasing anything online. LastPass is fully encrypted, so you don't need to worry about anyone stealing your information. If you want all of your passwords on your phone, download the LastPass iPhone or Android app.

17. WEBSITE CHAT: ZOPIM (FREE OR PREMIUM)

Zopim is a simple and cost-effective way to engage your website visitors with a live chat. This is a very effective way to engage potential clients who visit your site and may have a question about your services. Think about all those people who come to your site but never contact you. What are they looking for? What couldn't they find? Why did they leave? If it doesn't drive you crazy, it should. These could all be potential customers! Install Zopim in a few clicks, and now people can send you messages that go to your smartphone, or you can reply back by email when you're free. Have a full-time receptionist, secretary, or paralegal? Have them open up Zopim on their computer every day to answer your visitors in real-time. There is another solution that we recently discovered called ApexChat.com. They are actually real people trained in dealing with law firm clients, and they charge you per chat. The goal is to have them pre-qualify and bring in as many leads as possible, doing all the legwork and chatting for you. They don't mention pricing on their website, but someone I know using them says he pays $10/chat. It may seem a little pricy, but if you can convert 1/10 website visitors into a paying customer, is it worth $100 to you?

18. SOCIAL MEDIA MANAGEMENT: BUFFER (FREE)

Buffer is a great way to drive traffic and increase fan engagement on social media. You can schedule, publish, and analyze all your social media posts in one place without having to do it manually every day. Buffer also has tools to help create beautiful images in seconds, saving you time and money on hiring a professional designer to do it for you.

19. BUSINESS EMAIL: GOOGLE APPS FOR WORK (STARTING AT $5/MONTH)

Having a custom business email address not only makes you look more professional, but it also builds trust. Google Apps for Work gives you a custom email address with your domain name - for example, john@ watsonlawfirm.com. You can add and remove people anytime as your firm scales up and down. One of the hidden gems of Google Apps for Business is the communication features such as a shared calendar, Google Docs, and the full suite of Google products.

20. LOCAL MARKETING: GOOGLE MY BUSINESS (FREE)

If you use Google Maps, you should immediately look into Google My Business, formerly known as Google Places. Google My Business helps you list your law firm on Google Maps so potential clients can find out more about your business and location. Not only is this a good strategy in generating potential clients, but it also improves your SEO for your website. If someone is searching, for example, for a "Personal Injury

Attorney in Miami, Florida," Google will pull up the local results, some of which have Google My Business pages set up and verified.

21. LEGAL MARKETPLACE & DIRECTORY: AVVO (FREE OR PREMIUM)

Avvo is a very popular online legal services marketplace. Attorneys can link to their website; and show off their academic and employment history, publication credits, awards, and cases they've won in the past. One of the best features of Avvo is the Q&A platform. If someone posts a legal question in their forum, and you give a qualified answer, you have a much better chance of getting hired by that potential client. If used correctly, Avvo can be an extremely useful tool for marketing your firm and getting new clients.

TAKE ACTION

Now that you learned about these new tools, take action! Before you move on to the next chapter, write down the tools you want to learn more about. Then, set a time on your calendar to look into them and start free trials to see if you can incorporate them into your practice.

If you have any questions, don't hesitate to reach out to me at dbitton@practicepanther.com for any feedback or advice. And if you have other tools you'd love to share, or any integrations you would love to have with PracticePanther, I'd love to know about them!

LEARN HOW TO PREVENT OUTLOOK ISSUES BEFORE THEY HAPPEN

By Lisa Hendrickson

—

Lisa Hendrickson is an independent Microsoft Outlook, Office 365, and email migration expert. Ranked #1 in Google, her clients are worldwide, and include partners at law firms, IT departments, and anyone needing email help!

CHAPTER 17

Learn How to Prevent Outlook Issues Before They Happen

By Lisa Hendrickson

I've always had a love and passion for Microsoft Outlook, and I'm extremely happy to share the personal tips and tricks I've accumulated over the years. I'll be teaching you how to prevent Outlook issues before they happen, strategies to stop email overload, and actionable steps to getting the most out of Microsoft Outlook and Exchange.

For those who aren't familiar with Microsoft Exchange, it's a mail and calendaring server hosted by Microsoft. By creating an Exchange email address, you are able to create an email address with your domain name - for example, lisa@callthatgirl.bizcom. It also allows you to setup a business calendar where you can invite staff or clients to events and meetings. The best part is, you can get all your emails and calendars synchronized to your phone, tablet, and any of your computers with Microsoft Outlook.

TIP #1 - BACKUP, BACKUP, BACKUP.

This cannot be stressed enough with your email. Be sure you or your IT department back up your Outlook OST file. Outlook saves all your emails into files called an OST or PST file. If you're on a Windows PC, you can usually find them by going to your C Drive and navigating to the folder - C:\Users\user\AppData\Local\Microsoft\Outlook. Many IT departments don't believe it's necessary, but it really is. Back up everything regardless.

Be sure your email and all Outlook information are backed up, especially if you're using a POP email account, as chances are these emails won't be backed up anywhere online if your Outlook crashes.

Depending on which version of Outlook you have, click "File" on the top left of Outlook and select "Open & Export," then click the "Import/Export" button on the right. Select the option "Export to a file," and click "Next." Select "Outlook Data File (.pst)" and click "Next." Select your email address all the way on top, and click "Next." Lastly, choose a location to save your backup file and click "Finish." Go to that location on your computer where you backed up your file and upload that file to any online backup you have, like Dropbox, Google Drive, One Drive, etc. If you don't have any of these, copy this file to an external hard drive. If you don't have that either, I highly recommend you invest in either of these two options ASAP.

TIP #2 - ONEDRIVE OR DROPBOX IS NOT A RECOMMENDED BACKUP SOURCE.

If you're going to manually back up your files as described above, then OneDrive or Dropbox will be fine. I do not, however, recommend setting up a continuous automatic backup of your Outlook PST or OST files, because there is a high chance of the files getting corrupted. Outlook is constantly updating this file, and you will have OneDrive or Dropbox updating it as well. What happens if you have double-syncing and Dropbox syncs the wrong version back to your computer? Data corruption.

Here is how to disable OneDrive from your Windows 10 computer:

1. Press the Windows key on the bottom left of your keyboard, and the R key at the same time. This should open up the Run window.
2. Type in gpedit.msc and click OK.
3. Click the right arrow on the Administrative Templates folder to view all the subfolders.
4. Click the right arrow on the Windows Components folder.
5. Click on the OneDrive folder.
6. On the right, click twice on the option that says "Prevent the usage of OneDrive for file storage."
7. When the popup window opens, select the option on the top left that says "Enabled" and press "OK" on the bottom.
8. That's it!

TIP #3 - KEEP OUTLOOK SIMPLE.

- Don't over complicate your Outlook processes. Keep things simple and use fewer folders for your day-to-day work.
- Examples: Having too many tasks or categories, flags, rules, etc.

TIP #4 - KEEP ALL YOUR LOGINS AND PASSWORDS UP-TO-DATE.

- Have all your user accounts, passwords, and software in order in case of emergency.
- Know who manages your website control panel, as well as your email records.
- Know your website logins.
- Be sure to pay all the invoices for email hosting, website hosting, and all business tools for your communications and marketing.

TIP #5 - UPDATE YOUR SOFTWARE EVEN IF IT MEANS AN ADDITIONAL COST.

- Use up-to-date software, i.e., Outlook 2013 or 2016. Outlook 2010 is still a commonly used program, but it's very out-of-date and hard to repair. Upgrading is the best option and ultimately less costly.
- Some old versions are no longer supported and won't work with the new Office 365.
- Newer versions are supported by Microsoft with licensing, so some repairs will be at no charge – not all repairs, but many are, regarding the software itself.

TIP #6 - STOP USING FREE ONLINE APPS TO SYNC CONTACTS AND CALENDAR (E.G., ICLOUD AND OUTLOOK.COM).

- Using free synching software can cause data corruption, or - even worse - data loss. Their support is usually not up-to-date on how to find lost data, and this can cause you many hours of downtime and frustration.
- Use Exchange for syncing your calendars and contacts versus iCloud or free 3rd-party apps.
- Sync your contacts from Practice Panther using Exchange.

TIP #7 - TRAIN YOUR TEAM.

- If you hire someone new and they don't know Outlook, they should have training.
- Outlook is probably your main business application, and having a well-trained staff increases its efficiency and your productivity.

TIP #8 - ELIMINATE THE PROBLEMS OF: LACK OF EMAIL RESPONSES, FAILED CALL TO ACTION, AND MISSING EMAILS.

- Learn how to manage your inbox and move emails into folders. You just need to drag and drop your email into a folder on the left of Outlook. If you don't have any folders, you can right click on the "Inbox" folder on the left and select "New Folder." Just don't overdo it with folders, or it can get overwhelming.
- If you have a cluttered inbox, this is a sign of unmanaged email. Many people with inbox clutter never know when a day starts or ends. A sign of an unmanaged inbox is over 100 emails in it. If you have as many as 500 in your inbox, then you should consider inbox management training. If you have over 1,000, then consider hiring someone to help you with getting this down to a manageable level.
- If you often hear "Did you get my email?" or other comments about your lack of responses to email, you might have an inbox management issue.
- Emails with inboxes overloaded and sent items tend to "break" more often in Outlook due to overload.

TIP #9 - KEEP AN EYE ON JUNK MAIL AND SPAM.

- Be sure to check your junk and spam folders daily.
- Sometimes important emails end up in here because someone inadvertently wrote an email with a subject line that gets in the spam filter. You don't want to lose potential new clients because of something this easy to stay on top of.

TIP #10 - USE "RULES" FOR ORGANIZING EMAIL.

- Use Rules for any emails that you need automatically sorted to a specific folder.
- There is a limit of 50. Although some people can go over without a problem, you might come across an issue and rules will get corrupted.

Learn how to use junk filters more and Rule management to keep under the 50-rule limit.

- Keep in mind that Rules emails don't hit your inbox on your smartphone.

TIP #11 - MISCELLANEOUS TIME SAVERS:

- Use "Quick Steps" or "Rules." This will help you automate common or repetitive tasks like automatically moving an email into a folder based on the email sender, subject line, and more. Under the main "Home" tab of Outlook, you will either see "Quick Steps" or "Rules" with a dropdown menu. Click on it and select "Create Rule" to try your first one out.
- Use "Quick Parts" to create canned responses (email templates) you can use to quickly reply to emails. To create a new response, create a new email, type your canned response in the body of the message, highlight the text, then click the "Insert: tab. Click "Quick Parts," then "Save Selection to Quick Part Gallery." When you see the popup, type in the name of the response, and click OK. To test it, create a new email, click into the body of the message, click the Insert tab, select Quick Parts, and select the one you just created. Voila!

TIP #12 - HOW TO FIX OUTLOOK YOURSELF, AND WHEN TO GET HELP.

- When you have trouble with Outlook, be careful when Googling solutions. Not every answer you read on the internet has been proven to fix issues, and some may cause destruction to your data.
- Beware of downloads which may not be reliable or safe.
- If you are going to fix something yourself, backup the data beforehand just in case you break anything.
- Don't ever delete a profile in Outlook unless you are absolutely sure you have the data backed up.

TIP #13 - SYNC TO YOUR PRACTICE MANAGEMENT SOFTWARE.

- If you're using a practice management software, sync your emails over.
- This ensures another layer of backup, as well as the ability to run conflict searches from directly inside your practice management software. Most should be able to search through all the contents of your emails, as long as you sync them over.
- Ask if they have a feature to help you find all emails that have not been billed. This is a great way to bill your clients for every email you send. If you haven't already done so, I highly recommend charging your clients in 6-minute increments for every email and putting this in your retainer agreements. If not, many clients will take advantage of emailing you 1,000 times at all hours of the day and demanding immediate answers. If they understand that every email could potentially cost them money, they will be much more careful about sending off long rants at 2 AM, instead of bothering you for important questions pertinent to their case.

TIP #14 - ENSURE THAT YOU HAVE GOOD, DIRECT, PROMPT SUPPORT.

- When you are selecting a law firm software company, be sure their support department is responsive via telephone.
- When you have issues, you need to make sure you can call someone. Email is not the best support if your Outlook is down.

TIP #15 - IMAP TIPS:

- If you're using IMAP or Exchange, be sure that your email is managed well for the size of the mailbox; large mailboxes do not sync well with Outlook. It does work better with Exchange, but not IMAP.
- If your calendar and contacts show "This computer only," you will want to be sure that those are backed up manually, as those are "cached copies" and not able to be backed up.

RECLAIM YOUR WORKDAY WITH EVERNOTE

By Heidi Alexander

—

Heidi Alexander is the Director of the Massachusetts Law Office Management Assistance Program (LOMAP) where she provides free and confidential practice management assistance, guidance in implementing new law office technologies, and methods to attain healthy and sustainable practices.

CHAPTER 18

Reclaim Your Workday with Evernote

By Heidi Alexander

I am an attorney by training. I went to law school, worked at a small firm practicing employment law and litigation, and realized I was much more interested in the management side of the firm. So I left and started my own consulting practice. That is what led me to my current work, which I love, because I get to help attorneys figure out how to run their practices.

Most of the attorneys I've met would rather focus on the substantive aspects of the law rather than run the business. The latter is what I help attorneys with. I love talking about marketing and implementing technology to help attorneys keep up with all the rapid changes to the law and the legal industry.

This chapter will address the benefits of Evernote to running your practice. Evernote can be used in a multitude of ways and is highly complementary to case management programs. In this chapter, you'll learn what you can get out of Evernote and how to implement it in your practice. In addition, I'll provide tips and tricks to help you to use it like a "power user."

INSUFFICIENT SYSTEMS

Solo and small firm practitioners are constantly bombarded from every direction by a multitude of competing demands. Some of these demands come from clients, some come from colleagues and staff, and others from family. But of course, there is the actual work that you need to get done. On top of this, you must keep everything under control. However, most of us do not have the June Cleaver-like ability to juggle all these competing demands, keep a spotless practice, and leave everything perfectly organized when we clock out. But we can always strive to be better at it.

If the organization problems I deal with everyday were as simple as a few scattered papers, then I would be doing something else. In reality, most solo and small firms have much bigger problems when it comes to organization. Apart from forgetting to empty the recycling bin, I see lawyers struggling with cluttered inboxes, misfiled documents, and desktop screens covered with a jumbled mess of files and folders that make it impossible to track or identify one case from another. Let's be blunt: this is a malpractice claim waiting to happen.

A study from the Princeton Neuroscience Institute looked at what happens when you work in an environment that is cluttered and disorganized. They found that when your environment is cluttered or chaotic, it restricts your ability to focus. This is true of physical and virtual environments.

All the mess draws your attention away from what you really need to be focused on. You are bombarded with too many external stimuli, and it all becomes a source of stress. It creates the appearance that your work is never done, so you never achieve that feeling of accomplishment.

This is not all about physical distractions, either. The average person has 70,000 thoughts per day or about 49 thoughts per minute. There is also research out there that shows that we spend more than half of our day thinking about something other than what we are currently doing. So, what we need is a way to take all that stuff and get it out of our head, so that we can focus in on whatever it is we need to be doing, things like drafting that time-sensitive motion or returning the phone call of a potential new client.

The solution: Evernote. Evernote can help you clear up that clutter, both external and internal, and assist you in focusing in on the things that need to get done.

WHAT IS EVERNOTE?

Evernote is a note-taking program, a memory aid, and an organizational tool for your data. It allows you to collect all that data on your computer and stuff from your head and serves as the central repository for all that information. That way, you free up space in your mind so you can concentrate on what you need to be doing.

You can use Evernote to take notes, save articles, annotate documents, and since your data is stored in the cloud, it syncs up to all your devices so you can access it whenever you need it. Evernote is a tool that attorneys can, and should, use daily in their practices.

A LOOK INSIDE EVERNOTE-WORKSPACE

When you open up Evernote, you will see your workspace, which is a dashboard that provides all your tools to create notes and access notes, share and collaborate, and more. On the left-hand side, you can see a list of notebooks, shortcuts, and tags. You can customize how much of the workspace is viewed.

A LOOK INSIDE EVERNOTE-NOTES

As the name implies, notes are at the heart of Evernote. Your notes can contain text, audio, images, documents, emails, and web content. You can title the notes, write body text, and customize the style and format of the text.

A LOOK INSIDE EVERNOTE-TAGS

Evernote's notes are contained inside notebooks. But, unlike an electronic folder system with multiple levels of folders, Evernote provides only a single hierarchy. To organize them, tags are essential. Tags work well with the built-in search functionality, so you can access everything in your Evernote account within seconds rather than having to search through countless folders.

I might have case law involving employment issues in my "Employment Discrimination" notebook. To enable me to easily find this case again, I'll give it some descriptive tags like the name of the court or case proposition. Then, when I need a U.S. Supreme Court case on sex discrimination, I can search for those tags, and Evernote will pull up all that case law that I have saved and categorized with those tags.

A LOOK INSIDE EVERNOTE-SEARCHING

Evernote's search functionality is one of its greatest strengths. You can search within the contents of notes, search tags, search within attachments and images, within PDFs, and you can even search within handwritten notes. Let's say you scribble some notes during a meeting. Instead of typing the notes, you can take a picture of your notes and save them to Evernote. Then, when you search for some text within that handwritten note, Evernote should be able to find it. This functionality relies on built-in optical character recognition (OCR) that scans PDFs and converts the text into a searchable form.

There are many different ways to search within the system. You can search very broadly within your entire Evernote workspace, or you could search by notebook, by tag, or within a certain note.

EVERNOTE FOR ATTORNEYS

In this next section, I will share with you some of the ways in which attorneys specifically can use Evernote.

1. Save and Store Content

Attorneys need to store and access all different sorts of content in their practices. Evernote allows you to save and store all different content formats, including text, audio, images, and more. You can include text in a note as well as add audio files. You can also upload images, PDFs, and other attachments, such as word processing documents and presentations.

One of my favorite Evernote features allows you to open an attachment from a note, such as a Word document or PowerPoint, make changes in Word or PowerPoint, click save, and it saves right back into your note. This works because Evernote saves a local copy of your notes on your computer's hard drive. After you save your document, the changes are then synced to the cloud, thus obviating the need to continually drag, drop, upload, and download attached files to a note.

Evernote's mobile app enables you to snap a photo of a hardcopy document and save it to the app. Evernote can also be used to scan and save business cards. Attorneys collect tons of business cards when networking. But what do we do with all these cards? Well, either we trash them, lose them, or they sit on our desks forever. We may think about following up, but other things may get in the way, and suddenly we have more clutter.

Again, Evernote can help attorneys reduce that clutter. When given a business card or shortly thereafter, take out your Evernote app, create a new note, snap a photo of the card, and Evernote will automatically recognize that this is a business card. It will extract all the information on the business card and create a note for you in a business card notebook. Evernote can also save this information to your phone's contacts and automatically request a connection via LinkedIn. I know many attorneys who use Evernote for this feature alone.

Another unrivaled feature is Evernote's Web Clipper. By installing an extension to your browser and navigating to a site that you would like to either bookmark or save content from, you can click on that extension and it will save it right to Evernote.

There are a number of different formats you can use to save web content. For example, if you save it as an Article, Evernote will strip off some of the web formatting. If you save it as a Simplified Article, Evernote will strip it down to only text. You also have the options to select the notebook to save it in and add tags.

The Web Clipper also has a "Smart Filing" feature which allows Evernote to predict where you would like a saved web file to be placed. For instance, let's say you do a lot of legal research using Google Scholar and save cases from Google Scholar into your Evernote case law research notebook. The next time you save a case, Evernote will recognize that the content should be saved into a case law research notebook.

Furthermore, you can save content from email. If you have the Plus or Premium account for Evernote, you get a unique Evernote email address to send emails directly to your account.

If you have a Basic (free) account, you can still save emails to Evernote by using one of these workarounds:

1. If you use Gmail, you can use the aforementioned Web Clipper to save emails into Evernote.

2. If you use Outlook, when you download Evernote for your desktop, an add-on will be automatically added to your Outlook to enable you to save emails directly from Outlook. The image below shows you an example of how that works. You can select the notebook, tags, and add a remark that will appear at the top of the note.

2. Share Content

Evernote provides some great sharing and collaboration features. There are a few different ways to share and collaborate on notes.

1. Share Via a Public Note Link: You can share any content in your Evernote with a public note link. When you click the "Share" button at the top of a note, you can create a public note link that can be copied and sent to anyone with or without Evernote. The recipient opens the link in their web browser. The note will be viewed in real time, so if you make any changes to your note they will appear via the link. I use this feature often to submit articles to legal publications or send form samples to clients.

2. Share Via Email: You have the ability to share a copy of a note via email. For example, if you want to share your client intake form with a colleague but you do not want them to see any changes you make to the note later, you can send a static copy of the note. By doing it this way, your note will appear in the body of the email rather than in a link.

3. Share Via Work Chat: If you are working with other people who use Evernote, you can use the Work Chat feature to communicate and collaborate with them. For example, you can share a note with someone, and once a change is made to it, the change will be reflected on your own Evernote. However, unlike in a Google Doc where you can collaborate in real time, Evernote will lock the note once someone begins working on it to allow that person to make edits. There is also a history feature that keeps track of the changes made to your notes, giving you the option to restore any previous versions.

3. Firm Administration

It is essential that your firm has a central repository for all the administrative data within it. The image below is a sample firm administration notebook and a "notebook stack," which organizes your notebooks into specific groups. The stack is not a hierarchical system, which means I can't put notes into the general firm administration notebook; instead, I put notes into one of these seven sample notebooks. The notebooks stack serves essentially as a group heading.

Evernote, like many other electronic systems, sorts information alphabetically and chronologically, but special characters always take precedence. I've used intentional naming conventions – to force Evernote to sort this notebook at the top of the list. I have further organized my notebooks numerically to manually order these notebooks. This enables you to customize Evernote's view to suit your specific needs.

4. Marketing

Evernote can be used to organize your marketing efforts. For example, you can use it to keep an ongoing list of marketing ideas, draft blog posts, or keep track of information for networking purposes. Furthermore, if you find an advertisement or a website that you like, you can use the Web Clipper and clip it right to your "Marketing" notebook or an "Ideas" notebook.

5. Productivity and Time Management

Evernote also has some helpful features to keep you on task and save time. Evernote reminders allow you to add a specific due date to a note. That reminder will then appear in a section on the top of your notes. You can also set Evernote to send you an email when the reminder is due.

Because it is impossible to keep up with all the reading you need to (or could) do, you can use Evernote to capture information to read later. Save information from email using the Web Clipper ,and either organize them in a "Read Later" notebook or add a "Read Later" tag. When you have down time, all your reading is easily accessible.

Evernote also has a checkbox feature to create a checklist for specific tasks. For example, if you are filing a motion, you can have a checklist of everything you need to do. Thus, every time you need to file a motion you can replicate that checklist and use it as a template for filing the motion.

If you are a Getting Things Done (GTD) fan, Evernote is a great way to implement it. GTD is a method of time management created by David Allen.

6. Security

Keeping your information secure is top of mind for all attorneys. Thankfully, Evernote has great security features to help keep your information secure. A few highlights include the following: Evernote does not own your data; Evernote encrypts your data at rest and while in-transit; and Evernote allows for configuration of two-factor authentication.

However, since nothing is 100% safe, I will list a few steps that you can do to help ensure the security of your data.

- Strong Passwords: Use long multi-character passwords that are unique to each service you use. There are a variety of password managers available to help you safely keep track of your passwords.
- Two-Step Authentication: Turn this feature on in Evernote as well as with other cloud-based services, such as Google, Dropbox, etc. Two-factor requires you to enter both a password and a pin code before you can access your account. Therefore, if someone does gain access to your password, they would also need the pin code to access your account.
- Text Encryption: Many services like Evernote will encrypt information when it's sitting on the servers and encrypt it when it is in transit. That means that the provider does not own the data, but they do have the encryption code. If you want to prevent even Evernote from having access to your data, you can take an extra step and implement client-side encryption, i.e., only you hold the encryption key. If you have extremely sensitive data, such as a Social Security number or credit card number, you can use Evernote's text encryption feature to encrypt just that text.

Evernote is a brilliant piece of software that can be used by attorneys in a plethora of ways. Get started with the tips I've provided in this chapter and you'll be on your way toward a clearer mind and less chaotic practice!

CHAPTER 19

MICROSOFT WORD - QUICK TIPS

By Chelsey Lambert

—

Chelsey Lambert is Solo and Small Law Firm Technology Specialist, published Author and CLE Speakert. She is a former consultant and technology trainer as a Practice Management Advisor for the Chicago Bar Association. Today, she writes the legal technology blog LexTechReview.com.

CHAPTER 19

Microsoft Word – Quick Tips

By Chelsey Lambert

As professionals in the legal field, we spend more time in Microsoft Word than most people. Before reading this chapter, pull out your computer so you can practice these tips while reading. The following power features will help you break through some of life's daily formatting headaches and breeze through documents with ease.

For extra credit, add each of them to your Quick Access Toolbar located at the top left corner of your screen to shave off a few more seconds during the drafting process. It will be extremely hard to remember what I teach you without practicing right away, so let's get started with your computer open!

FORMAT ERASER

I like to call this feature the 'Magic Eraser,' a tool that will save you days over the course of a year. If you find yourself fighting with text or need to reset formatting for an entire section, this tool is your new best friend.

1. Select the text or graphic that has the formatting you want to erase.
2. If not already selected, click on the "Home" tab on your ribbon.
3. In the "Font" section, there will be a "Clear Formatting" icon. It is a letter "A" with an eraser in front. Click it to erase the format.

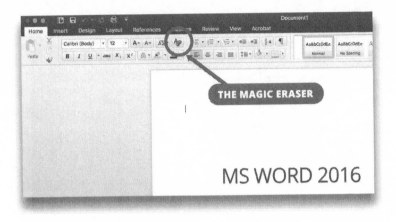

THE MAGIC ERASER

MS WORD 2016

SHRINK TO ONE PAGE

This feature is utilized to avoid printing a whole page of white space when you have only a small paragraph, rows of a table, or text that bleeds over into the next page. The feature "Shrink to Fit" or "Shrink to One Page" automagically resizes the text, adjusts margins, and brings everything together to fit on one page.

1. To get to the "Shrink One Page" command, open your "Quick Access Toolbar." You can do this by using the down arrow above the tabs on your ribbon, usually the last icon. Select "More Commands." OR, click on the "File" tab on your ribbon, select "Options," and then select "Quick Access Toolbar" on the left-hand side.

2. Once your "Quick Access Toolbar" dialog box is up, under "Choose Commands From," choose "All Commands." Scroll down through the list of commands until you find "Shrink One Page."

3. Click "Shrink One Page" to select it, and then click "Add."

4. Click "OK."

5. A new icon should show up above the tabs on your ribbon. Click it to shrink the text.

STYLES - HOW TO APPLY A STYLE TO TEXT

Styles are the fastest way to format a document. Once you get the hang of using the basic styles that are already set up for you in Microsoft Word, you can move on to create templates for your law firm that will save everyone on your team hours per week!

1. Select (highlight) the text that you wish to change.
2. If not already selected, click on the "Home" tab on your ribbon.
3. In the "Styles" section, click the style you wish to apply to the selected section. (Note: If you want to see more styles, click the "More" drop-down arrow found in the bottom-right of style options.)

STYLES - HOW TO APPLY A STYLE SET

If you have been using headings and styles in your document and you'd like to change everything over to a new style all at once, there are some great options in the "Design" tab!

1. From the "Design" tab, click the "More" drop-down arrow in the "Document Formatting" group.
2. Choose the desired style set from the drop-down menu. The selected style set will be applied to your entire document.

STYLES – HOW TO MODIFY A STYLE

To modify an existing set of styles, you just right click on any style in your library and follow the directions below. Don't overlook the option to save the settings as a template to create a standardized document your whole team can use!

1. Locate and right-click the style you want to change in the "Styles" group; then select "Modify" from the drop-down menu. A "Modify Style" dialog box will appear.
2. Make the desired formatting changes, such as font style, size, and color. If you want, you can also change the name of the style. Click "OK" to save your changes.

STYLES – CREATING A NEW STYLE

1. If not already selected, click on the "Home" tab on your ribbon.
2. Click the arrow in the bottom-right corner of the "Styles" group. The "Styles" task pane will appear.
3. Select the "New Style" button at the bottom of the task pane. A dialog box will appear.
4. Enter a name for the style, choose the desired text formatting, and then click "OK."
5. The new style will be applied to the currently selected text. It will also appear in the "Styles" group.

USING HEADINGS TO BUILD A TABLE OF CONTENTS

A professional Table of Contents makes a document immensely more functional, both as a Word version and as a PDF. If you've been using styles, this process is quick and easy to do!

1. When typing your document, make sure to apply a "Heading Style" to the title for each separate section.
2. Click in your document where you want to create the table of contents. If you'd like it to appear on its own page, insert a page break (Ctrl+Enter) before and after inserting the Table of Contents.
3. Click the "References" tab on your ribbon.
4. Click the "Table of Contents" icon in the "Table of Contents" section.
5. Choose which style Table of Contents you would like and select it. Word will create a Table of Contents from the document text you styled with one of the first three heading styles: Heading 1, Heading 2, and Heading 3.
6. Note: Hold Ctrl and click on one of the page numbers to navigate to that location in the document.

LINE NUMBERING

For court documents or any other drafting that requires line numbers, the built-in "Line Numbering" tools are fast and easy to use.

1. Click the "Layout" tab on your ribbon.
2. Click "Line Numbers" in the "Page Setup" section.
3. Word gives you four options to choose from. If you don't want any of

these, then open the "Page Setup" section, either by clicking the arrow in the bottom-right corner or clicking "Line Numbers" and go to the bottom option, "Line Numbering Options." The "Page Setup" dialog box will open.

4. Make sure the "Layout" tab is selected. Click on "Line Numbers" at the bottom middle of the box. This will open a "Line Numbers" dialog box where you can customize your line numbers.

Note that every line is counted except for those in tables, footnotes, endnotes, text boxes, and headers and footers.

Let's face it, you're probably using Microsoft Word at least 10% of your workday, if not far more. By mastering Microsoft Word, you will save a considerable amount of time and make your documents look significantly more professional than the law firm next door. I recommend going to your computer and trying out the tips and tricks before moving onto the next chapter. If you have any questions, feel free to reach out to me anytime by sending me a message from http://lextechreview.com/contact/. I look forward to hearing from you soon!

EVERYTHING YOU NEED TO KNOW ABOUT E-DISCOVERY

By Eddy Bermudez

—

Eddy Bermudez grew up in Miami, Florida and went to graduate school at the University of Chicago where he studied postcolonial and feminist literature with an emphasis on food studies. He also worked as an Adjunct Professor for both Miami Dade College and St. Thomas University and a Lecturer for the University of Miami.

CHAPTER 20

Everything You Need to Know About E-Discovery

By Eddy Bermudez

One of my favorite novels is William Gibson's sci-fi cyberpunk masterpiece, *Neuromancer*. In the book, hackers "jack-in" to cyberspace (Gibson's book popularized the term) and explore massive, shining cities of data that represent the internet. Our world is some time away from Gibson's vision of hacking, but the massive cities of data he describes are no longer in the realm of fiction.

Consider how many emails you get every day. Massive amounts of data are created daily. I have previously written about how law firms must adopt new technology to grow and succeed. E-Discovery is a vital part of the legal process, and lawyers need to know how to navigate these shining cities of data.

E-DISCOVERY: AN OVERVIEW

Electronic discovery (a.k.a., e-discovery, ediscovery, eDiscovery, or E-Discovery) is a part of the normal discovery process. In the past, the parties involved in a legal dispute would exchange relevant information in the form of physical documents. Today, documents are increasingly generated digitally, requiring a fundamental change in the discovery process.

Thus, the "E" in E-Discovery stands for electronic. E-Discovery is the process by which parties share, review, and collect electronically stored information (ESI) to use as evidence in a legal matter. ESI is a broad term that can encapsulate a whole host of digitally created content.

Emails, Microsoft Word documents, social media posts, company-specific databases, and audio and video files all fall under the domain of ESI.

The E-Discovery process is long and complex. It begins as soon as litigation is foreseeable, at which time attorneys from both sides will find and preserve the relevant ESI and make E-discovery requests and challenges. It is important to preserve the original content to avoid claims of evidence tampering. The ESI is placed on a legal hold while attorneys and paralegals search for relevant documents.

Attorneys can use e-Discovery software, like Computer Assisted Review (CAR) or Technology Assisted Review (TAR), to cut the time and cost of the review process. Either software can sift through a multitude of documents and help attorneys find the ESI relevant to the case. Coupled with the automation features provided by legal case management software, attorneys can simplify the E-Discovery process and do their work faster and better.

Once the relevant documents are selected for production, they can be converted to a format like a PDF and presented in court. ESI is so valuable to attorneys because it can offer the key piece of evidence to win a case.

WHY DOES E-DISCOVERY MATTER?

Simply put, in the very near future, e-Discovery will be essential for an attorney to provide competent representation. In fact, amendments to the Federal Rules of Civil Procedure (FRCP) have already been made to recognize E-Discovery as a vital procedure for civil lawsuits. The most common malpractice claims are the result of simple laziness or bad recordkeeping on the attorney's part. We will soon have to add inexperience with e-Discovery to that list.

As the scope and volume of ESI intensify into the shining cities of data Gibson envisioned, attorneys will have to become experts at navigating these cities like the hackers in Neuromancer. This means that attorneys and other legal professionals will have to learn new technical skills. A defensible e-discovery process will make strange bedfellows of attorneys and IT professionals.

Furthermore, E-Discovery work is increasingly being done in-house. In the past, many E-Discovery tasks were outsourced to third parties. Post-recession, the trend is to save money by bringing the work in-house. Moreover, E-Discovery software (like the two mentioned before) are making the in-house review stage of the e-Discovery process much more cost-effective, meaning that unless an attorney is willing to shell out a lot of cash, they cannot escape ESI. The only solution is to avoid foot-dragging. Attorneys should take steps now to familiarize themselves with the E-Discovery process.

HOW TO USE E-DISCOVERY

Tip #1: Learn the Process

Thankfully, legal professionals can use the Electronic Discovery Reference Model (EDRM) as a starting point. The EDRM is widely considered the definitive framework for the E-Discovery process. The EDRM divides the E-Discovery process into nine iterative "stages" (meaning one might repeat the same step multiple times) connected by arrows. What follows is a summary of the stages.

- **Information Governance (IG):** IG is the process of getting your shining house of data in order to mitigate risk and expenses. As companies create, collect, and store more data, they must consider how to keep that data secure, private, and compliant. From creation to deletion, IG is about getting companies to create and carry out a series of procedures for how they create, manage, store, and secure ESI. This also includes the legal and regulatory obligations tied to E-Discovery. IG even has its own model for legal professionals to follow: The Information Governance Reference Model (IGRM).
- **Identification:** In order to prepare for litigation, the legal teams need to identify and decide what pieces of ESI are relevant.
- **Preservation:** Relevant ESI cannot be destroyed or altered. This is usually done through a legal hold sent to the custodians of the data informing them not to delete certain ESI.
- **Collection:** ESI must then be gathered for processing, review, etc. with no alterations to the ESI.
- **Processing:** The collected ESI must be prepared for attorney analysis. To help reduce the volume of data, specialized software is used.

- **Review:** This stage involves evaluating ESI for relevance and privilege. Software like Computer Assisted Review (CAR) or Technology Assisted Review (TAR) can distinguish between relevant and non-relevant documents.
- **Production:** Produce relevant ESI as evidence following court rules and procedures.
- **Presentation:** The last step is displaying ESI as evidence in a trial, deposition hearing, etc.

Tip #2: Be Thorough

When collecting data, be as comprehensive as possible. Everyone involved in the legal dispute should be interviewed, and any relevant insights or information should be collected from them. They should also be made aware of the hold that is placed on the information they offer. Maintaining the original content of the ESI should be a priority for all attorneys.

Tip #3: Be Aware of Your Data Collection Options

Since ESI is so broad and the data can come from varying sources, the forensic technologies used to collect the data can be overwhelming. Figure out which process works best for you (and your bottom line). Whichever tools you use, ensure that the data is collected comprehensively, with attention paid to its authenticity and the preservation of the chain of custody.

Tip #4: Keep Track of Every Step of the Process

Document every step of the collection process. Create a system that documents every step of your process and use it for every case. You may also consider hiring a third-party to audit your process.

Tip #5: Focus Only on What Matters

The sheer amount of data that can be collected during the E-Discovery process is staggering. However, the majority of this data is useless. Your priority should be to focus on the data that is relevant to the case. An attorney can save significant time and money by using technology to cull irrelevant data for them. As such, plan out the scope of the case early on so you can figure out the precise timeline and type of data you require.

Tip #6: Make the Review Process More Efficient

The review process has typically been done through keyword hits. This process is very inefficient, so adopt a contextual review process to save time and costs. Use E-Discovery software to cut the review time and organize the information. This type of software can help sort through a multitude of data, like email chains, and organize them so they can be presented in context.

Tip #7: Communication Between Parties Is Crucial

In order to avoid last-minute emergencies and additional work, the parties involved in the case should agree upon the production details, limitations, and other technical details early on. The same goes for the team you will work with (whether it is in-house or a third-party). Be clear about who is responsible for the production work and make sure they understand the production requirements.

Tip #8: Track and Evaluate all the Production Documents

Track both paper and electronic documents and who handles them as they go through the processing and discovery processes. As soon as you receive any data, conduct a review to note what you received and your assessment of the data. Frequently review all the data to make sure no privileged files are shared with opposing counsel.

While at times complex and arduous, the E-Discovery process is an unavoidable part of the larger legal process. Attorneys cannot afford to lag behind, especially when the consequences can be as severe as lower profits - or worse, a malpractice or bar complaint. Attorneys need to take the time to review the appropriate materials on e-Discovery and become experts in the EDRM model. Those cities of data are waiting to be traversed. Make sure you know your way around.

—

PROTECTING YOUR FIRM

3 REASONS WHY YOUR FIRM NEEDS TO "IT-UP"

By Eddy Bermudez

Eddy Bermudez grew up in Miami, Florida and went to graduate school at the University of Chicago where he studied postcolonial and feminist literature with an emphasis on food studies. He also worked as an Adjunct Professor for both Miami Dade College and St. Thomas University and a Lecturer for the University of Miami.

CHAPTER 21

3 Reasons Why Your Firm Needs to "IT-Up"

By Eddy Bermudez

Whether 'tis nobler in the mind to suffer through all the bad things luck throws at you, or to take arms against all those things that trouble you by putting an end to them? Yes, I am being a bit pretentious. But Shakespeare's words are relevant here. How do you deal with the day-to-day challenges of running your firm? Should you put up with it or do something about it? Simply put, if you want your firm to grow, you have to take action. A legal IT consultant can help solo and small firms put an end to the challenges that are keeping them from being competitive with larger firms.

WHY YOU ARE HESITATING, HAMLET?

I understand even a tech-savvy lawyer's time is better spent being a lawyer than updating a website. Moreover, it does not matter if you have the latest software if no one can use it properly. So, who is going to train your employees to use the shiny and new technology? Setup, implementation, and training are all major time-killers. And then add this to every other challenge that comes with running a firm.

The goal is to get lawyers back to practicing the law. This cannot be done without directly tackling the things draining your time. The fact is, technology can and will make your life easier and save you time. A legal IT consultant will use their ability to take some of the weight off your shoulders. Let them handle all your technology needs, freeing up more time for you to get back to your clients.

BRING AN OBJECTIVE EYE

I get it, Hamlet. Your firm is your baby. You have invested a lot of time and money in it. You want your firm to succeed, so it is hard to trust someone else with it. But this is exactly what makes an IT consultant so beneficial. Sometimes, you are too close to something to see it objectively. An IT consultant is a neutral party. Vital changes will be made by someone who is objective. Most IT consultants are not "yes" men or untrustworthy. You should be able to trust them to give you their fair thoughts on how to improve your firm.

You may already be using technology like case management software. However, one of the most common ways you waste billable hours is with bad software. You may choose your current software because a sales rep gave you a good pitch. It is difficult to realize why your current software is not saving you time without testing each one yourself. This trial-and-error process is just too time-consuming.

An IT consultant is not a salesperson. You can trust that they will recommend the best case management software for your needs. An IT consultant will learn what you and your staff need out of the software. They can assess which software meets those needs and ask the right questions to a salesperson. This process could take you weeks to complete on your own. Your consultant will handle the grunt work. You do not need to divide your time between cases and trial software.

SAVE TIME AND MONEY

Training also is not an issue when you have an IT consultant. Lawyers tend to stick with bad software because it is inconvenient to train themselves and their staff in new software. The consultant will choose software that is the easiest to use and direct training themselves. Again, this is another task you do not have to deal with. You also save time spent on training, getting schedules in order, and implementing the new software. Overall, this is a much less stressful process for you and your staff.

IT challenges do not end after you install all the fancy hardware/software. We can look forward to AI solving this problem for us one day, but not yet.

IT consultants stick with you until the needed changes are complete. IT consultants do not just make suggestions and leave the rest to you. An IT consultant will develop a long-term strategy and work with you on how/when to best to make changes. There is no need to ask a ghost for advice. You can rely on regular updates from the consultant to make sure they are meeting goals.

Therefore, the most important part of an IT consultant's job becomes to reclaim your billable hours and personal time. You have a dedicated professional handling all IT issues and implementation of new technology for you. Your firm can only grow if you are doing your job and helping your clients. The IT consultant eliminates the extra work that is important for growing your firm, but distracts from your billable hours.

Moreover, as you begin to add more technology, you (or someone) will also have to keep up with updates and changes. This is a difficult task even for fresh-faced lawyers. Technology is simply advancing too quickly to consistently stay up-to-date. Very few lawyers can dedicate the necessary time to keep up with all the changes, work with their clients, run their firm, and complete other tasks.

The IT consultant's job is to keep up with the pace of change and trends. They will update your firm and guide you and your employees through those changes. Likewise, the shiniest, newest technology is seductive. IT consultants know what will work best for your firm. They will recommend only the technology your firm needs. You can rest assured that money is not being wasted on useless tech. The consultant will give you a detailed explanation on how/why the recommended changes will meet your firm's needs.

MEET GOALS WITH LESS STRESS

One of the biggest challenges to meeting goals are employees. You should be able to trust your employees to do the jobs you hired them to do. Employees, however, hate to have new tasks added to their workflow if they need to learn new skills. Employees are resentful of having to do a task they have little experience with or knowledge of. This creates extra stress on them and slows down the progress of their work. You cannot blame them for this. IT consultants realize it is a lot to ask of employees to add more duties to their plate.

An IT consultant will use their knowledge and resources to help your employees as well. The consultant does not simply train employees to use new technology; they also serve as a guide and teach skills. The IT consultant will come up with a plan for helping employees adapt to their new tasks. This is especially helpful considering how multigenerational firms are becoming. Some employees will adapt quicker to their new tasks. The consultant will create specific schedules and strategies for these employees. Once the employees understand the changes, they will feel less resentful of the new work. This relieves stress and work gets started sooner. Thus, the IT consultant saves time and money in the short and long run.

There is no excuse not to take action. You should hire a legal IT consultant because they will help you grow your firm. Take your rightful place as king of all firms. The rest is silence.

HOW TO AVOID THE MOST COMMON MALPRACTICE CLAIMS

By David Bitton

—

As an author, CLE speaker, and founder of PracticePanther.com, David is dedicated to automating law firms with the help of today's technology. He's revolutionizing the legal industry by helping lawyers get more done in less time using PracticePanther's practice management software.

CHAPTER 22

How to Avoid the Most Common Malpractice Claims

By David Bitton

Malpractice claims are shockingly simple to get, but yet quite easy to avoid. According to a malpractice expert who performs risk assessments for insurance companies, the highest risk factor – and thus the most expensive malpractice insurance policy – is for small firms with two to five total attorneys. The larger the firm, the lower the risk, as they have better processes, procedures, workflows, paralegals, and secretaries checking every detail for you.

The good news is, all of these processes and procedures are being detailed in this book for attorneys in any size firm, sole practitioners, new lawyers, "old" (a.k.a. "dinosaur," as one author called them) lawyers, tech-savvy lawyers, or even lawyers with a flip phone – who are about to trade that in for a smart phone, right? As long as you take action on most of the advice you're learning, you should be in a much better place than you were before you picked up this book.

According to the American Bar Association's publication of Profile of Legal Malpractice Claims from 2008-2011, these are the top 10 practice areas with the highest risk of claims:

Rank	Practice Area	Number of Claims	Percentage
1	Real Estate	10,772	20.33%
2	Personal Injury – Plaintiff	8,260	15.59%
3	Family Law	6,432	12.14%
4	Estate, Trust, & Probate	5,652	10.67%
5	Collection & Bankruptcy	4,876	9.20%
6	Corporate/Business Organization	3,597	6.79%
7	Criminal	2,996	5.65%
8	Business Transaction Commercial Law	2,176	4.11%
9	Personal Injury – Defense	1,727	3.26%
10	Labor Law	1,160	2.19%

If your primary practice area is in the upper half of that chart, you should be aware that you have a much higher chance of getting a malpractice claim, and thus you should start preparing for how you can protect yourself and avoid future claims. But as you can see, every practice area - every attorney - is susceptible.

According to the same Profile of Legal Malpractice Claims, but from 2000-2007, the following were the top 10 most common allegations of error (i.e., legal malpractice):

Rank	Malpractice Claim	Percentage
1	Failure to Know / Apply Law	11.3%
2	Planning Error	8.9%
3	Inadequate Discovery / Investigation	8.8%
4	Failure to File Documents / No Deadline	8.6%
5	Failure to Calendar Properly	6.7%
6	Failure to Know Deadline	6.6%
7	Procrastination	5.9%
8	Failure to Obtain Client Consent	5.4%
9	Conflict of Interest	5.3%
10	Fraud	5%

At quick glance, it appears that most attorneys get malpractice claims for failing to know the law, or to help their clients correctly. But when taking a deeper look at numbers 4, 5, and 6 on the list, it actually is a problem with deadlines and calendaring. A whopping 24.1% of malpractice claims are from missed or inaccurate deadlines on your calendar!

After thorough research and investigation, it appears that most lawyers are adopting the exact same process for finding deadlines:

1. Looking up deadlines on Google.
2. Calculating the number of days by hand or with the help of their calendar.
3. Researching local and national holidays to take into account.
4. Updating deadlines if court rules change.

After speaking to many attorneys and experts, the problem seems to lie with miscalculating deadlines, failing to update deadline dates after a court rule has been changed, and simply forgetting to calculate the deadline or put it in their calendars with reminders.

I can't help you with failing to know the law, inadequate discovery, and definitely not fraud, but I can give you some guidance and advice on how to avoid the other seven errors leading to malpractice claims.

#1 – AVOIDING PLANNING ERRORS & MISSED DEADLINES

We now know missed deadlines are, overall, the most common source of malpractice claims. We also probably know there are many ways to miss a deadline: you forgot, you had the wrong date, you procrastinated. Some lawyers make the mistake of thinking that working towards a deadline is the best practice. Not true. You are working for your client and you should do everything to meet their best interests.

Luckily, this one is actually quite an easy fix, and for relatively low cost as well (starting at $49/matter or $39/person/month and going down from there). I'm going to reveal one of the best kept secrets not many people know about – a solution that actually calculates all your deadlines for you and even schedules them directly on your calendar. That solution is a website called LawToolBox.com. With an IP patent, they are one of the only programs that actually has almost every court rule in every jurisdiction across the United States. (Apologies to our international readers!) I know this was mentioned in a previous chapter, but here it is again in more detail.

How does it work? You simply select the jurisdiction, select a trigger date (i.e. the date your client was served or the date you received a notice from the court), and it will automatically calculate all the upcoming deadlines for you. It also takes into account business days, weekends, and local and federal holidays. If the court rule changes, it will automatically update in your calendar. The best part is, they integrate with Microsoft Outlook, Office 365, SharePoint, Google, iCal, Apple, PC, and even a few practice management platforms. Once you connect it to the program of choice, it will add all the deadline dates to your program for you. Make sure to also set up reminders by email or SMS if it's a very important deadline.

By the way, some malpractice insurance companies will even give you a discount if you tell them about how you handle deadlines and what programs you use to automate the process. Make a note of this and remember to contact your insurance company to see if you qualify. You're welcome.

#2 – COMMUNICATING WITH YOUR CLIENTS

The 8th most common reason for a malpractice claim is "Failure to Obtain Client Consent" – in other words, lack of communication. Just like in marriage, you must have strong, consistent communication with your clients.

According to ABA Model Rule 1.4 on Communication, it states that a lawyer:

1. "Shall explain a matter to the extent reasonably necessary to permit the client to make informed decisions regarding the representation.
2. "Shall promptly inform the client of any decision or circumstance with respect to the client's informed consent, as defined in Rule 1.0(e).
3. "Reasonably consult with the client about the means by which the client's objectives are to be accomplished.
4. "Keep the client reasonably informed about the status of the matter.
5. "Promptly comply with reasonable requests for information.
6. "Consult with the client about any relevant limitation on the lawyer's conduct when the lawyer knows that the client expects assistance not permitted by the Rules of professional Conduct or other law."

Put yourself in your clients' shoes. Wouldn't you want to know what's happening with your case? Wouldn't you want to make educated decisions based on facts and the law? Wouldn't you want to feel like you're in control, and help the lawyer make the right choice that could potentially affect your life? It's no secret; this is exactly what your clients want!

Before you go into a retainer agreement, I highly recommend finding out if the client can even afford your services, as well as if you can dedicate the required time to their case. You don't want to take on a matter, only to realize it's going to be a waste of time for you.

If you feel like your clients are expecting the world from you and want you to be available 24/7, you need to set better expectations. If you're having these issues (or actually, even if you're not yet), I recommend letting them know every phone call or email will cost them money and be billed in 6-minute increments. Make it very clear that you have specific office hours and will respond to any calls or emails by the next business day. (And, of course, then do so, even if just in the form of an assistant responding that you are in court or otherwise unavailable, but that as soon as you are free, you will be getting back with them.)

If you do not want to be available on weekends, let them know that as well. By the way, all of these guidelines should be put into your retainer agreement, agreed upon, and signed by the client. Do you expect your doctor or dentist to answer the phone every time you call, or be available to speak five times a day? You can lay the groundwork for your clients to have these same expectations (or lack thereof) - if you want to, of course.

More importantly and as addressed above, you, your paralegal, or a virtual receptionist need to be available to answer and return clients' calls, especially if they're requesting more information about their case. Anytime there is an update, your clients should know about it, and there should always be a record of the client being informed. Email is usually best, as they can always claim they never received your phone call.

If you use a CRM software, or even an Excel spreadsheet, make sure you set reminders to follow up and communicate with your clients on an ongoing basis. Even if nothing is happening in the case, it's always best to check in and let them know you're on top of everything. The worst thing that can happen is have your client think you're not doing any work or thinking about them. And insult is added to that injury when they receive a bill for services they were unaware were being rendered.

#3 – CONFLICT OF INTEREST

Conflict of interest accounts for 5.3% of all malpractice claims. If a lawyer is materially affected by the matter and puts his/her own interests before that of his/her clients, this is something I cannot help with. To be blunt, that is an open, obvious (to the lawyer) conflict which requires no conflict check, and if there is a violation, it is intentional. This book is not intended to address such complaints.

However, if you take on a case that can potentially affect your professional duties and responsibilities towards a current or previous client, or even have the appearance of doing so, this is a problem that can easily be solved. I strongly believe a major cause of inadvertent and unidentified conflicts of interest is most law firms not being paperless, as well as not using any software or database to keep track of all clients and related entities. I recently asked a room of fifty attorneys how many of their practices were paperless, and only two hands went up.

I'm curious and would love to be enlightened as to the procedure of doing a conflict search when you have a five-hundred square foot room filled with filing cabinets and tens of thousands of documents. It's virtually impossible to go through everything.

To do an absolutely thorough, foolproof conflict search, you should probably be doing the following:
1. Search through all of the emails ever sent in the entire law firm, across everyone's inboxes.
2. Search through the phone notes and call logs of every person in the firm.
3. Search through every task, event, meeting, hearing, or case you've ever had.
4. Run a keyword search across every document ever scanned in.
5. Search through all the names of every client, matter, case, judge, opposing counsel, and anyone you've ever worked with.

I'm taking a wild guess that virtually no one does this. Who could *possibly* have the time or resources to do so? Well, we all do! It is actually quite easy to accomplish and should drastically reduce the number of conflicts you have, as well as the risk for potential malpractice claims.

All you need is a system that allows you to manage everything. There are two options I have in mind that can help you do this:

1. Practice management software – Obviously this was going to be on the top of my list, and in my biased opinion, it is by far the easiest way to get everything in one central location. You simply sync your emails to the software, sync with your document management platform, and voila - everything is in one central system. Just make sure everyone in your firm is taking very detailed notes on every call, time entry, task, and event. When it's time to run a conflict search, just

type in any name to the search box, and search through everything including your contacts, matters, notes, time entries, tasks, events, emails, calendar events, and more. Imagine, what once took you hours (if you were doing it correctly), can now take a matter of seconds.

2. You could upload all of your scanned files to Google Drive and search through them as well. You could use Google Contacts and search for any contacts or notes. You could even create Google Docs and Sheets for any notes, phone calls, and tasks, which can also be searchable. If you have multiple people in the firm, you could even have everyone forward all of their emails to one main email address that could be used just for conflict searches. It sounds a bit crazy and will take a lot more work, but this is probably the best free solution I could come up with.

Either way, find a solution that works for you, and start implementing it as soon as possible. If you have another creative solution to running conflict searches, please shoot me an email! dbitton@practicepanther.com

#4 - KEEP A PAPER(LESS) TRAIL

Lastly, the seemingly menial work that comes with running a solo or small firm can really often be the most important. If you don't have a good system to manage your files, it is so easy to miss deadlines, overlook conflicts, and develop poor relationships with your clients, all of which can result in costly malpractice claims or extremely stressful bar complaints.

There is just no reason why you should have to spend hours keeping track of or looking for files. Do some of you more "seasoned" lawyers remember the days of a staff person misfiling something – either a document in the wrong client's file, or an entire file not where it belonged? Those things immediately became needles in a haystack.

Find a system that can help you store, back-up, and keep client information secure. This will ensure that your documents are always at your fingertips, and that you have an efficient and reliable system to cross-check case information. This can help you avoid miscommunication and stay protected if your hard copies are ever lost, also avoiding resulting malpractice claims. Further, it can save you and your staff so much time that could be better spent serving your clients (or relaxing on the beach). Like I mentioned in a previous chapter, invest in a Fujitsu ScanSnap ix500 scanner. You'll be happy you did!

As we've learned, technology is increasingly becoming an invaluable tool against malpractice claims. You can avoid so many common yet costly errors if you follow the tips provided here and use the features included in your practice management software, or a program like LawToolBox - or both, if they integrate together. If you have any other innovative ways to prevent malpractice claims, I'd love to know about them. Send an email to **dbitton@practicepanther.com** and we can chat. Stay safe, and stay compliant!

AVOIDING COMMON BILLING MISTAKES AND FEE DISPUTES

By David Bitton

As an author, CLE speaker, and founder of PracticePanther.com, David is dedicated to automating law firms with the help of today's technology. He's revolutionizing the legal industry by helping lawyers get more done in less time using PracticePanther's practice management software.

CHAPTER 23

Avoiding Common Billing Mistakes and Fee Disputes

By David Bitton

Do your best to make sure you never get involved in a fee dispute with a client. Keeping clients happy is not just about providing quality service and results, but also ensuring your fees are fair and your billing is professional and transparent. Most clients' biggest fear is how much they will pay. They're always afraid of getting a massive invoice at the end of the month. Before they hire you, make it crystal clear how much it should cost. If possible, set maximums, which gives clients some sense of certainty. All timekeeping, fees, transactions, and payment details should be clearly documented to avoid any conflict. You should never have to do unpaid work or sue your client for unpaid fees.

DEFINE YOUR TIME PROPERLY

It's easy to fall into the trap of working all day, getting distracted, and then guessing how many hours you worked. To make matters worse, some attorneys write a short description of what they worked on all day, not providing the client with any transparency. This is actually fairly common among less experienced attorneys and firms, but it can cast doubt into the mind of your clients. By lumping tasks together, you may give the impression that you are hiding inefficient practices, or worse, overcharging.

The easiest way to define and manage your time is by keeping a detailed record of what was done and at what times. You can use Excel, Google Sheets, or a case management software to keep track of this. Whatever method you choose, make sure not only that you are not over-billing the client, but that you are not under-billing, either. We find that many attorneys actually don't bill enough, giving many freebies away like phone calls, emails, short meetings, text messages, and more. If you have an app on your computer or phone that can quickly start a timer, that would be ideal. The most important thing is to always track your time accurately and provide detailed logs.

TRACKING BILLABLE EXPENSES IS ESSENTIAL

Expenses are a common inclusion on legal bills, but it's easy to lose track. Clients more than ever want to see exactly how their money was spent. If they suspect a single dollar has been spent on expenses that weren't necessary, then a fee dispute might occur.

If you use a practice management software already, make sure to download the iPhone or Android app, take pictures of every billable expense and receipt, and upload it to the client's file. All of this information can be turned over to the client when providing an invoice, or if you're audited one day.

It's also wise to discuss with your client how much money will be used from their retainer payment to pay any third-party expenses. Fee disputes are far less likely when the client has agreed upon a timeline, a price, and general expenses, and it's in writing.

AVOID DELEGATION AND MULTI-BILLING

It's easy for a senior attorney to use a paralegal to help with a case, but when a client is paying senior attorney fees, it becomes not only unethical, but fraudulent. Avoid falling into this trap and properly organize how you will manage a case. If a paralegal will be involved in fulfilling certain milestones, simply include this on your planning documents and adjust the fee accordingly. If you're using a case management software, this is as easy as selecting another person when adding a time entry, and it should automatically calculate their personal hourly rate.

Multi-billing, whereby a number of attorneys appear at the deposition and regularly work on a case that can be handled by one attorney, is another cause for concern. In some cases, this might be necessary, but in the event that it should have only required one attorney, a fee dispute is likely. It's essential that a client is given the services that they need and no more – unless they specifically ask for it.

ARRANGE A SIGNED FEE AGREEMENT

A signed fee agreement is a document that outlines what a client will pay. Typically, these documents are provided not only to ensure a client pays only for what they agree to, but also to set out provisions in the case of unexpected events. For instance, expenses and general overhead costs will be outlined, but provisions will be made in the agreement if more than one attorney is required to work on the project.

Specific circumstances can be laid out in the fee agreement, whereby more attorneys, or staff members, begin working on the case. This puts the client's mind at rest, knowing that the case will only cost them more than expected if A) an unexpected event occurs or B) they agree to involve more people to improve their chances of success.

A signed fee agreement may also outline any retainer fees that might be necessary. These agreements are beneficial for both parties, helping you avoid fee disputes and ensuring you maintain your reputation while also giving clients the best insight into what their case will cost.

USE A CLIENT PORTAL & EVERGREEN ALERTS

If you have a client portal through your practice management software, show it off. Let your clients know they will be able to log in to your client portal from your website, and view how much money is still in the trust account and how much has been paid so far. They should even be able to view all previous and pending invoices if you allow them. Trust me, they will love the transparency. You should also ask your software company if they have an "evergreen" retainer feature that will automatically notify you if the trust account balance goes below a certain dollar amount. This way you will know that the client's retainer needs to be replenished before further work is done.

If you find yourself having billing disputes with a client, always take a step back, calm down, and think about how you can prevent it from happening again. Every bad experience can be a learning one.

Take these tips you've just learned and apply them to your law firm. The worst thing you can do is put this book down without taking any action. You just learned the keys to avoiding malpractice claims and billing disputes; make me proud and put them into action!

HOME MAC, WORK MAC

By Tom Lambotte

—

Tom Lambotte is the CEO of GlobalMacIT, a national Managed Service Provider providing complete end-to end legal technology services to Mac-Based law firms. They maximize profits and productivity to attorneys using Apple technology by leveraging technology.

CHAPTER 24

Home Mac, Work Mac

By Tom Lambotte

Many attorneys who use Mac devices use them both at work and at home. This means that your business Mac, iPhone, and iPad often do double-duty as your personal Mac, iPhone, and iPad. How do you keep your attorney-client privileged documents and confidential business records separate from your awesome selfie collection and world-class cat video library? How can you keep your family photos apart and distinct from your pictures of the accident site survey? In this chapter, I'll touch on the biggest concerns regarding using a laptop for both home and work. Although the article is Mac-centric – since that is our niche – the same benefits and concerns apply to PC users.

In this first section, we will discuss the biggest benefits for the law firm as well as the end users. The second half of this chapter will address the biggest security concerns and provide strategies to address them. Let's dig in!

BENEFITS FOR THE FIRM

Many firms who adopt a Bring-Your-Own-Device (BYOD) approach to technology reap the advantages of greater employee satisfaction, reduced IT costs, and faster device upgrade cycles. The technology your employees are using is more likely to be current. This means not only faster hardware, but more up-to-date software, including everything from new features to the latest security fixes.

BYOD can save your firm money: Instead of absorbing the total cost of a new Mac, iPhone, or iPad, most BYOD firms split the cost of the new device between the employee and the firm. This reduces the hardware cost to the firm and gives the employee extra incentive for properly maintaining their device. This approach does have the potential downside that an improperly monitored device - i.e. one with overly-permissive permissions or lax installation restrictions - can be a gateway for nefarious code to get onto other employee or firm computers, the removal of which can be expensive.

Employees can use devices with which they're familiar, hence becoming more productive faster. When it comes to people and technology, they are only going to use the technology available to them to the degree that they are comfortable and confident using it. Many of us have been positively surprised at one point or another when a parent or grandparent says, "Let me Google that." Why did they never embrace technology until they got that iPad or iPhone? Because they were not confident or comfortable using it. When your employees are able to continue using the devices they already interact with on a daily basis, it makes their learning curve much less steep. If an employee has one less thing to become competent at in a new job, they obviously become more productive in less time.

BYOD can lower your IT expenses, and it will certainly lower your hardware expenses. It's also possible that software expenses can decrease because newer equipment will ship with the freshest, most secure software.

BENEFITS FOR END USERS

Life happens. Kids get sick. Cars break down. Inclement weather blows through. Acts of God wreak havoc. Whatever you call it, it is inevitable that something will happen which keeps you from making it into the office. It is not a matter of whether this will occur or not, or even when, but the biggest issue is: What will happen when it does? Unfortunately, filing dates don't care about your life situations. The show must go on.

For those without BYOD policies who may only have a virtual private network (VPN) to access the office, it can be very difficult to work from outside the office. You'd be amazed at how many people who supposedly have a VPN solution never use it because it's either broken, unreliable, or so painfully slow they only use it in the direst situations. When mobile devices are properly configured and able to access firm email, contacts, calendars, firm files, and case management and billing software, employees are able to do almost 100% of what they need to do at the exact same speed.

Here's a client's experience with getting fully set up on Macs and being fully mobile:

> **"By converting my law firm from Windows to Macs, what GlobalMac IT has done for my ability to live my life and law practice, has been remarkable.** For instance, I am in Paris and my secretary is up in her cabin in the middle of nowhere. She is tethered to an iPhone, and my partner is home with a sick kid in Minneapolis. Yet, we are all doing business at a high level; it is instantaneous."

- Robert Hajek, Hajek & Beauclaire

This is night and day compared to many shoddy VPN connections available to employees.

Most people's computer training goes like this, "Congratulations, you have the job, here is your computer, get to work." Now, at this point in the employer/employee budding relationship, usually the new employee is not comfortable saying, "Oh, by the way, I've never worked on a Mac/PC/ tablet or this operating system before. Can you show me how to use it?" So they end up doing their best to figure it out, suffering in silence, very often to the detriment of their productivity. When an employee is allowed to use their own device, they already have a certain level of comfort using it, so they can ramp up faster.

Another benefit to the end user is that it allows them to decompress. People should be able to check out of work and go into personal things when needed. When your home Mac is also your work Mac, you can easily switch hats when you need to. Let's imagine you're traveling out of town for a deposition, you've been working all day, and just spent three hours after dinner prepping for the next day. You want to unplug and decompress. So you log into your photo album and spend some time cleaning up vacation photos to share with your extended family. You check into Facebook and screen-suck a bit to unwind. Without this, you'd have to travel with two laptops, which simply wouldn't happen.

As you can see, there are many benefits to all parties to embrace a BYOD policy. However, this strategy does introduce some unique security concerns you will need to properly address.

SECURITY CONCERNS AND STRATEGIES

Let's consider the biggest security risks, as well as some tips on how to address them. Given that GlobalMac IT only supports Mac-based law firms, this article will be Apple-centric, but the same concerns apply if you are on Windows-machines (although the specific tools will therefore vary). The three biggest concerns are the proper legal documents to have in place, full disk encryption, and securing your backups. This is in no way comprehensive, but here are some of the big ones.

First on the list is legal documentation. The purpose of a Mobile Device Management policy (a.k.a. BYOD Policy) is security, not employee monitoring. It should in no way be intrusive and overbearing, but rather practical and easy to enforce. I'm sad to report that only 31% of respondents to the 2015 ABA Legal Tech Survey had an employee privacy policy enacted and even fewer had a Mobile Device Management policy in place. This experience has been confirmed with our clientele when taking over their IT needs. In fact, I would say the percentage is far lower with smaller firms.

Who needs this document in place? Anyone allowing firm data to be accessed by any type of mobile device - phones, tablets, and yes, laptops as well. If you'd like a template to start with, shoot me an email at tom@globalmacit.com and I'll send you one to use as a starter. Not doing your due diligence here greatly threatens the attorney-client privilege and legitimately jeopardizes your firm (legally and otherwise).

The next on this list is using full disk encryption. Why is this necessary? Unlike a standard password-protected computer, which leaves the contents of a hard-drive accessible to anyone with the patience to remove the drive, FileVault encrypts the entire contents of a device at the disk level, rendering it impossible for anyone without the login password to access the data on the computer. To be clear, just because you have a password on your laptop does NOT mean the data is secure if you do not have this enabled. Anyone could open your computer, remove the drive and plug it into another computer, and have FULL ACCESS to EVERYTHING. This is also one of the reasons everyone has been moving to the cloud, as no data is physically stored on your actual computer's hard drive.

Apple has made hard drive encryption the default setting for every new Mac as of 10.10 Yosemite. Ticked by default are two boxes: "Turn on FileVault disk encryption" and "Allow my iCloud account to unlock my disk." That means that unless the user actively declines the offer, their hard drives will be encrypted. To check this status, go to System Preferences > Security & Privacy > FileVault. You'll see here if it has been enabled or not. If not, enable it and make sure to store the recovery key where you won't lose it! (See suggestions in other chapters herein.)

The third and final security is the security of your backups, not something often discussed. Similar to the full disk encryption, many home users will have a local backup hard drive that they use. Many Mac users use Time Machine due to its simplicity. Several others like making a bootable clone, which is a bit-by-bit copy of the entire hard drive. The same issue we just discussed applies here and can threaten your law firm. If you have firm data on your computer, go home and back it up. If that backup drive gets into the wrong hands, you've got a serious security issue. You are responsible for finding out how people in your firm may be backing up the computers at home and whether it is being done securely.

Just like FileVault on the Mac, Apple has added the ability to encrypt the entire Time Machine backup. Go to System Preferences > Time Machine > Select Backup Disk. On that window is a checkbox, "Encrypt Backups." For the clone, there are a few more steps. Carbon Copy Cloner is one of the most popular cloning applications and our preferred tool. The full instructions for enabling encryption on the backup volume for the clone can be found here: https://bombich.com/kb/ccc4/working-filevault-encryption.

I hope this has raised a few security concerns you may not have previously considered. More importantly, I hope you will take some action steps to improve the security in your firm and to ensure you are doing your due diligence to protect the attorney-client privilege when you or your staff are using mobile devices for business and personal tasks.

If you have any Mac related questions, feel free to reach out to me anytime at tom@globalmacit.com. I look forward to hearing from you soon.

BONUS CONTENT

Thanks to our legal experts, we are giving away
over $300 worth of free content!

WHAT YOU GET:
1. 10 Video Tutorials to Start, Grow, and Market Your Firm.
2. Free CLE Classes on Security, Copywriting, & Automation.
3. Access to Chelsey Lambert's paid courses.
4. Steve Fretzin's video tutorials with legal rainmakers.

Redeem your free bonus by going to:
https://practicepanther.com/book/bonus

FREE EBOOK DOWNLOAD

Download the eBook version for free by going to:
https://practicepanther.com/book/download

ADDITIONAL RESOURCES

The following is a list of resources provided by some of the contributors to further your growth and success.

21 Productivity Tools for Lawyers:
https://www.practicepanther.com/productivity-tools

Webinars with Legal Industry Experts:
https://practicepanther.com/webinars

Microsoft Word Keyboard Shortcut Cheat Sheet:
https://learn.lextechreview.com/microsoft-word-shortcut-cheatsheet

50% Off Chelsey Lambert's Microsoft Word Training:
https://learn.lextechreview.com/wizardry-in-word-for-legal-professionals
(use coupon code PRACTICEPANTHER)

Free CLEs on Security, Copywriting, Automation &more:
https://www.practicepanther.com/CLE

ACKNOWLEDGEMENTS

This book wouldn't have been possible without the help of the contributing authors and legal industry experts. You've dedicated your lives to helping attorneys, and we are grateful for sharing your knowledge with the world.

A special thank you goes out to Eddy Bermudez for helping organize and edit the early drafts, and to Laurie Aames for polishing the final product you see today with meticulous detail.

This book wouldn't have looked so nice without the help of the most talented art director I've ever met in my life. We are incredibly lucky to have David Puente on our team. Thank you for formatting the book, designing numerous covers, and always working hard to ensure the best-looking designs possible!

To Ori Tamuz, the greatest co-founder anyone could ever ask for. Thank you for helping us test and experiment with new ideas, teaching us to work hard, while having fun in the process, and maintaining the best work environment and culture. Thank you for always providing the best logical advice and feedback. You are a true role model to everyone in our company.

We wouldn't be here if it wasn't for my parents and Ori's parents guiding us through life. Thank you for always pushing us, believing in us, and helping us grow as individuals and business owners. Thank you for teaching us to always do the right thing in every situation, and to always be open, transparent, and honest with each other and our customers.

And last but not least, none of this would have been possible without the love and support from my wife Ilana, and Ori's wife Netali. Thank you both for staying by our sides after all these years of sleepless nights. Your feedback and guidance as two attorneys have been invaluable throughout our journey. We couldn't have done it without you.

ABOUT PRACTICEPANTHER

Co-founders David Bitton and Ori Tamuz set out to create the most intuitive, easy to use, and secure practice management platform so you can automate your firm and get more done in less time. PracticePanther is now used by thousands of solo, small, and medium sized law firms in over 35 countries worldwide. By combining time tracking, billing, payment processing, expense management, calendaring, and more, lawyers are saving hours each week managing their practice.

Work from anywhere, on any device, with the iPhone, iPad, and Android apps. Integrate with Gmail, Outlook, Office365, Exchange, Google Calendar, QuickBooks Online, LawPay, Box.com, Dropbox, Zapier, an open API, and more. Get world-class support by phone, email, or live chat. It's simple, user-friendly and intuitive. Now you can spend less time managing your firm, and more time making money.

We invite you to try PracticePanther risk free, no credit card needed. If you decide PracticePanther is the best fit, get 15% off your first year when using coupon code: AUTOMATEMYPRACTICE

Learn more at: **www.PracticePanther.com/book-deal-15-off**

ABOUT THE AUTHOR

DAVID BITTON

David Bitton moved to Miami, Florida from Port Washington, New York in 2002. He studied business management and computer information systems at the University of Miami and later worked at a high-growth startup software company.

As an author, CLE speaker, and co-founder of PracticePanther.com, David is dedicated to automating his life, and law firms with the help of today's technology. Before PracticePanther, David founded 3 music entertainment and computer service businesses. He was a state champion tennis player, who now spends his days with his wife Ilana, daughter Jamie, and Samoyed Dog Nala.

Made in the USA
Lexington, KY
04 March 2018